Epistemic Virtue and Doxastic Responsibility

Studies in Epistemology and Cognitive Theory
General Editor: Paul K. Moser, Loyola University of Chicago

A Useful Inheritance: Evolutionary Aspects of the Theory of
Knowlege
  by Nicholas Rescher, University of Pittsburgh

Practical Reasoning: Goal-Driven, Knowledge-Based,
Action-Guiding Argumentation
  by Douglas N. Walton, University of Winnipeg

Epistemology's Paradox: Is a Theory of Knowledge Possible?
  by Stephen Cade Hetherington, University of New South Wales

The Intellectual Virtues and the Life of the Mind: On the Place
of the Virtues in Epistemology
  by Jonathan L. Kvanvig, Texas A & M University

Blind Realism: An Essay on Human Knowledge and Natural
Science
  by Robert F. Almeder, Georgia State University

Epistemic Virtue and Doxastic Responsiblity
  by James A. Montmarquet, Tennessee State University

Epistemic Virtue and Doxastic Responsibility

James A. Montmarquet

Rowman & Littlefield Publishers, Inc.

ROWMAN & LITTLEFIELD PUBLISHERS, INC.

Published in the United States of America
by Rowman & Littlefield Publishers, Inc.
4720 Boston Way, Lanham, Maryland 20706

British Cataloging in Publication Information Available

Library of Congress Cataloging-in-Publication Data

Montmarquet, James A.
Epistemic virtue and doxastic responsibility / James A.
Montmarquet.
p.   cm.
Includes bibliographical references and index.
1. Responsibility. 2. Belief and doubt. 3. Virtue I.
Title
BJ1451.M647   1992   170—dc20   92-20272   CIP

ISBN 0-8476-7763-X (cloth : alk. paper)

Printed in the United States of America

The paper used in this publication meets the minimum requirements of
American National Standard for Information Sciences—Permanence of
Paper for Printed Library Materials, ANSI Z39.48–1984.

Contents

Preface

This study makes three central claims. Let me introduce these and briefly comment on each:

> I. Moral responsibility for what we do is often—although not by any means always—dependent on epistemic responsibility for what we believe.

Beliefs typically serve to justify, at least in the agent's own mind, what he or she does. In fact, even in cases of what is otherwise bad conduct, one's action may well be entirely blameless viewed in *relation* to one's beliefs (i.e., on the assumption that nothing was objectionable about these). So, for instance, the conduct of a *racist* may be unobjectionable relative to his beliefs. Still, in such cases we regard that conduct as morally wrong and, barring special circumstances, its agent as morally culpable. My question, then, becomes this. If we are to hold the agent culpable for his actions in such cases, must we not hold him culpable for holding these *beliefs*?

> II. Such doxastic responsibility is typically direct—although not complete. It is not, in general, derivative of responsibility for action.

This brings us to the heart of the matter. Many philosophers will readily concede that we bear a kind of *indirect* responsibility at times for what we believe—indirect because it depends on a more direct responsibility for relevant actions (and omissions of action). The main problem, however, with this indirect view is that it fails to push the issue far enough. Suppose that an agent does culpably fail to take some epistemically needed action (e.g., fails to look for more evidence in support of her opinion, when more evidence is clearly required).

Notice that typically in such an instance she will *believe* that no more evidence is required. Thus, if the argument alluded to earlier is sound (claim I), if we are to hold her culpable for omitting to look for more evidence, we must hold her culpable for believing that she needn't so look. Moreover, if the latter culpability is to be made out in terms of some *further* action or omission—she failed to check to see whether her belief that further checks were unnecessary was really justified—I will argue simply that we are on the road to a regress.

> III. Doxastic responsibility is based on the capacity we have to control—to a very real, if limited, extent—the exercise of certain qualities of epistemic character, the "epistemic virtues and vices."

The fundamental epistemic virtue—what I call (epistemic) *conscientiousness*: the desire to attain truth and avoid error—has been widely recognized by philosophers interested in the notion of "epistemic responsibility." But this quality, I try to show, must often be supplemented by one or another "regulative virtue," such as impartiality or intellectual courage, lest it express what is not a very virtuous intellectual personality at all. An extreme dogmatist, for example, may qualify as "conscientious"—as desirous of attaining truth and avoiding falsehood—without qualifying overall as epistemically virtuous; he may, for instance, be entirely closed-minded. On this account, then, the epistemic virtues turn out to be qualities that a truth-desiring person would *want* to have, but they are not limited to the latter desire itself.

To the above I would add here just two further points, by way of indicating just how the epistemic *virtues* on this account tie up with responsibility for *belief*:

> IV. The exercise of these qualities in belief formation or retention (e.g., by way of being "careful" or "conscientious" in what we believe) is not a mode of indirect, but a mode of direct influence over belief.

Just as "cutting carefully" is not a matter of performing some inner act (of "being careful") that indirectly affects one's outer act of cutting, believing "carefully" or "conscientiously" are ways of accomplishing *one* thing in a certain way. These represent *aspects* of the belief acquisition and retention process that are subject to our direct control even as other aspects of this same process are not thus subject to our control. (Hence, the claim, stated earlier but not commented on, that our doxastic control is always "incomplete," but not always indirect.)

V. This capacity to exercise qualities of epistemic character is not something we are simply free to exert when we wish, and even less something that we are capable of exercising at all times. Rather, it manifests itself as a *response* to particular situations in which we attach special importance to being correct in what we believe.

There is, to this extent, something right in the view which understands responsibility for belief in terms of responsibility for action. Typically, we are responsible for what we believe in just those situations in which it *matters*, for purposes of action, what we believe. But this is not because responsibility for belief is derivative of responsibility for action. Rather it is because our direct responsibility for being virtuous in what we believe consists in our responding appropriately to the differing demands of particular situations.

❋   ❋   ❋

The upshot of these claims is to present a somewhat different view of the nature of our responsibility for belief, and of its relation to our moral responsibilities regarding action, than many philosophers today seem inclined to accept. For the effect of these claims is to place our responsibility for what we believe in a *coordinate*, rather than a subsidiary, relation to our responsibilities for what we do. This is not to say—even if I am entirely right—that *all* moral responsibility is ultimately doxastic, a matter of our responsibility for what we believe true. The latter is a possible and perhaps a defensible philosophical position. (It would be a consequence, for instance, of the Socratic view that we will act rightly just in case we clearly see what is the right thing to do; for in that case, insofar as there is any blame for misconduct, presumably it is rooted in blame for not clearly seeing the right act, thus, not holding an appropriate belief.) But, again, I make no such sweeping claim. I claim only that doxastic responsibility is typically separate from and not based on its actional counterpart and that, often, the latter does turn out to depend on the former.

Now most contemporary thinkers (and many noncontemporary ones) reject, or would reject, such notions of "doxastic responsibility." They would do so, in the main, because they hold that this kind of doxastic responsibility entails an objectionable notion of "doxastic voluntarism" or "voluntary control" of belief. This inference, however, is mistaken. For my notion of a direct control of one's beliefs needs to be distinguished from an objectionable notion of direct *voluntary* control where the latter implies anything like a power to believe whatever one likes (or a power to believe that *p* "at will"). A power to exert certain qualities of epistemic virtue as modes or aspects of the process of coming to believe, or continuing to believe, *p* is very different from the power to believe *p* at will or simply because one wants to believe it.

A second difference with some contemporary authors should perhaps also be noted here. Unlike such current authors as Ernest Sosa (1985, 1991) and Jonathan Kvanvig (1992), I do not treat (most) *any* truth-conducive characteristic as an epistemic virtue. One reason for this is that I want to restrict the virtues to qualities for whose exercise or nonexercise we can plausibly be held responsible (praiseworthy or culpable). For another, I want to treat the epistemic virtues as, more narrowly, the counterparts of the moral virtues—and not just the counterparts of any personal characteristic (e.g., intelligence) that may be thought conducive to morally desirable ends. The effect of such positions as Sosa's and Kvanvig's, it seems to me, is to reduce "virtue epistemology" to something like the reliabilist epistemology of Goldman (1986) and many other contemporary authors. And this is deeply puzzling. Why introduce the entire notion of an "epistemic virtue" if this is not to place something like a special normative role in one's epistemology? (See in this regard the discussion of "normative epistemology" offered in Appendix 2.)

※ ※ ※

I thank Crispin Sartwell and Clem Dore, without whose helpful discussions of these topics this book would not have been possible (even if another, an inferior one, would have). I also thank Robert Audi, at whose NEH seminars I, with many other (once) young philosophers, became greatly interested in the problems of contemporary epistemology. Without Professor Audi, not only this book, but arguably *any* other book by me on epistemology would never have been written. Finally, I thank Paul Moser, editor of the series in which this book appears, for his encouragement and patience with a young manuscript that greatly needed further work. (Relatedly, I thank Professor Moser's reviewer, whose comments greatly shaped that further work.)

As this project began to near completion, I was greatly saddened to learn of the death of Alan Donagan, who supervised my dissertation at the University of Chicago and whose lively, analytical approach to issues of mind, action, and morality I have sought through the years, in my own less incisive way, to emulate. It is in his memory that I offer this book.

Chapter One

Arguments for Doxastic Responsibility

My main concerns in this chapter are twofold. First, I will want to argue that persons are at least sometimes responsible for their beliefs, and second, I will want to begin to clarify the basis of this responsibility. Responsibility for one's beliefs ("doxastic responsibility") is *not* derivative of our responsibility for action; it is more basic than that. Such responsibility, I will *begin* to argue, pertains to the responsibility each of us has for our "epistemic characters," or at least for the exercise, on certain occasions, of qualities of epistemic character. Which qualities and which occasions will be a matter, however, for later discussion (chapters 2 through 4).

1. The Problem Defined

Let us begin with this consideration. There are times when we want to hold an agent morally to blame for conduct which, from that agent's *own* point of view, seems quite justified. Cases in point abound, including many of the murderous activities of tyrants, terrorists, racists, and religious fanatics, not to mention the less murderous activities of plain self-righteous hypocrites. It would be an understatement to say that we are wont to cast "moral blame" on these individuals and their conduct, even when we are aware that *they* regard themselves as having done nothing wrong. But how are we entitled to cast such moral blame and even fairly to punish these individuals unless we can sometimes find these individuals culpable for having these beliefs in the first place?

Thus take the case of an Adolf Hitler. From the standpoint of *Hitler's* beliefs, all sorts of morally outrageous actions will have seemed entirely justified. In fact, they would have seemed justified to almost anyone holding Hitler's background beliefs.[1] To be sure,

1

some of Hitler's acts and policies remain immoral—even relative to this background—for some of these would still constitute plain excesses. But many other acts and policies of his *would* qualify as morally acceptable from the standpoint of Hitler's beliefs and their assumed soundness. (We shall consider soon enough what epistemic status—"true," "justified," "known to be true"—we must assume these beliefs to possess for them to render his conduct acceptable. So, for now, I mark time with the term "soundness.") Consider, then, such notions as the existence of a worldwide Jewish-Bolshevik conspiracy, headquartered in the unlikely nexus of Wall Street and the Kremlin, led by the vilest of men, and bent on the subversion and enslavement of the world. Now if this *were* known to all to be true, presumably some fairly drastic measures would be in order. If it were true that this conspiracy were extremely powerful, clever, well-financed, and widespread and that only immediate action could stop it, who can say just how much of the Nazi program would be defensible? (Analogously, the critics of Senator Joseph McCarthy would hardly have been well advised to concede, for whatever reason, the soundness of his beliefs about the extent of Communist infiltration of the United States.)

But even if, what is clearly false, nothing of the Nazi (or the McCarthy) program would have been justified relative to their beliefs, surely certain acts and policies—acts and policies that would *otherwise* have been completely unjustified—would have been justified (and seemed entirely so to their perpetrators). And that is enough to make my point. For there will remain morally culpable acts that would apparently be justified, and thus certainly not culpable, relative to the beliefs in question. My question, then, is this with respect to such acts: If we cannot assign culpability for holding such beliefs, how can we assign culpability for acts premised on their (assumed) truth?

Now there is a feature of the Nazi case and of all those under discussion, that, although it does not strictly concern me, bears mention because it has been a subject of some recent philosophical discussion. This is whether, in such cases, we want to blame the agent *merely* for her culpable beliefs (assuming, for the moment, that there is such a thing as a culpable belief) or whether, perhaps, we want to assign a separate judgment of culpability to the actions or for the effects of the actions to which these beliefs have led her. Michael J. Zimmerman (1988), for instance, has held that an agent is culpable for an action only if he takes that action in the belief that it is morally wrong.[2] As if to moderate a bit this rather bold claim, Zimmerman does allow that if one is culpably ignorant of the wrongness of one's action, one may be responsible for the ill-effects of one's ignorance, but one is still not culpable for the act itself (cf. p. 80). Holly Smith (1983) takes, on the whole, a more moderate view, suggesting only that if culpable ignorance leads one to perform some injurious act, no separate blameworthiness attaches to the act (as opposed to one's ignorance) as long as the act was not motivated by a "reprehensible configuration of desires and aversions" (p. 556). (Notice then, an action, say, motivated by hate may be blameless by Zimmerman's lights, although not by Smith's.) I shall discuss some of Smith's views in chapter 4, but what concerns me here is not whether blame attaches merely to one's belief, to one's action based on that belief, to the effects of one's action, or to some combination of these. It is just this: If we are to attach blame *at all* to agents in the cases to which I have alluded, I will want to argue that we must hold them culpable for their beliefs. Whether we want to hold them culpable in anything like a separate way for their actions or the effects of those actions is not something which will concern me.

The general direction of my argument may now be indicated. If we are to cast moral blame on an agent in a case where what he did would have seemed quite justified to him (or to most anyone else holding his beliefs), I will need to show that we must find this individual culpable for having these beliefs. To do this, however, I will clearly need to defeat two contrary suggestions. First, it might be acknowledged that the agent's fault in these cases is indeed rooted in the defectiveness of his beliefs but it might be insisted that such a demonstration of defectiveness is enough to impute moral blame—without any imputation of responsibility for these beliefs themselves. Second, it might be claimed that the agent's real fault (for which she genuinely was responsible) did not lie, except in an entirely derivative way, in her beliefs at all but instead in something else: namely, her failure to take appropriate *actions*, presumably by way of verifying her beliefs.

2. Truth, Justification, and Responsibility

What ways might there be of "attacking" or "impugning" a belief without any corresponding attribution of responsibility? Certainly one such mode of attack would be to show that a belief was simply *untrue*. Thus it could be urged that it is enough to know that Hitler's main beliefs were untrue to safeguard our moral condemnation of his actions. But such a position is clearly indefensible if this condemnation is supposed to support a judgment of Hitler's moral culpability. Inasmuch as the issue here is one of culpability, of *blaming* someone for something, it is just implausible and entirely at variance with our ordinary procedures in assigning fault to base this on questions of truth as opposed to such more limited notions as the information available to Hitler and what he should have believed given this information. If Hitler's beliefs were true but he altogether lacked any reason for thinking them so, presumably this would at most mitigate his moral guilt. If, conversely, Hitler's relevant beliefs were entirely false but he had every reason for thinking them true, presumably this would more considerably mitigate his guilt, if not entirely *justify* his conduct. In short, the idea is that, both in commonsense morality and in the law, we judge individual conduct not so much according to the truth, as the grounds, of the beliefs on which that conduct is founded. (Thus, in the case of the moral and legal status of self-defense, the issue is not whether one's belief that another constituted a threat to one's life was true; it is whether this belief was reasonable.)

But if it is not enough to show that Hitler's beliefs are untrue, may it perhaps be enough (enough to lay an adequate foundation for his moral blameworthiness) to show that they are *unjustified*, although not in any sense that implies responsibility for his holding them? Unjustified, but in what sense? For our purposes here, current accounts of epistemic justification may be distinguished according to the conditions they place on what shall serve to justify a given belief. For the internalist, such justifiers must be factors internal to the person—presumably beliefs of this individual. For the externalist, no such restriction is made.[3] So let us consider each notion of justification, as applied to our problem of epistemic justification and moral responsibility.

The basic externalist idea, applied, say, to the Hitler case, would be that whatever principles and processes Hitler used to arrive at his (wrong-headed) beliefs may be safely judged quite unreliable, quite unlikely to produce true beliefs. From this base, then, one could claim that any acts premised on the truth of such beliefs are unjustified. Insofar as Hitler's actions are founded on such unjustified beliefs, an externalist could say, they may be judged morally wrongful, and insofar as Hitler is responsible for these wrongful acts, he may be judged morally culpable for them.

This, however, is mistaken. Consider an agent, Mary Smith, who performs an action based on a perceptual belief that she has every reason for thinking true, but that is false, owing to some undetectable breakdown in her visual cortex. Mary thinks that the figure charging toward her is a hostile stranger; however, it is actually her husband. Mary's belief, we are supposing, is unreliably formed, and, by the externalist's lights, unjustifiable. Now suppose that Mary takes some action that would have been entirely correct and commendable, had her perceptual belief been correctly (and reliably) formed. Mary drops the assailant with a solid right cross. How, then, does the unjustifiability of her belief affect the moral evaluation of her act? Surely, Mary is no more culpable for this act (even based as it is on an unreliably formed belief) than she would have been for stopping a genuine assailant, not unless it can be shown that she was in some measure negligent or otherwise to blame either in forming the belief or in checking the belief or in acting on the belief that this charging figure was an assailant. The point is really quite simple. Without a finding of *fault*, there is no culpability; mere unreliability is not, is not as such, a fault. Thus, reverting once again to the Hitler case, we can see that (in the relevant cases of actions that would have been justified had his beliefs been justified), if Hitler's only epistemic shortcoming was that his beliefs were not reliably formed, this would be an inadequate basis for any judgment of moral culpability for those actions.

We need, then, a conception of "good epistemic behavior" different from the externalist's to ground our ordinary notions of moral responsibility. But before we launch any further search for such a notion, let us briefly remark on the import of this last result. Certainly, one plausible test of a conception of epistemic justification is its "fit" in such cases as Mary's with our notion of moral justification. To claim that Mary is not (epistemically) justified in her belief but is (morally) justified in acting on that belief is, one suspects, a dubious undertaking. For it is surely plausible to say that part of what it is for a belief to be epistemically justified (or unjustified) is for that belief to provide an epistemically proper or (improper) basis on which to act. Insofar as the externalist's view must deny this connection—and hold that a supposedly unjustified belief such as Mary's can provide an epistemically proper basis for conduct—I think that the externalist has an implausible view of epistemic justification.

We shall return to such topics in more detail much later in this study (sections 6.2–6.3); for now let us proceed to the internalist's view. An exponent of this view could assert in the present connection the following:

First, in the case of Mary Smith, I would hold that she *was* justified in her belief that the man coming her way was a hostile assailant—briefly, because she had no reason to think otherwise and because she had every reason to think that this was so. But in Hitler's case I claim that no such epistemic justification was available. He had every reason to think that these absurd notions of his were *false*. After all, he had access to much the same general information about the world as other politically interested people of his place and time. He was, during the crucial early years of his adulthood, a citizen of Vienna and an avid reader of many of the same journals and newspapers that nourished his political adversaries. A lack of access or exposure to information about the world was not Hitler's problem, but the fact was that he effectively disregarded this information and whatever doubts it cast on his own system of beliefs. Or let me put the point in this way: I agree that a finding of moral culpability in this case requires, and derives much of its plausibility from, a finding of epistemic fault. What I reject is the thesis that such fault requires a special, presumably voluntarist, notion of doxastic responsibility. Evidently, it requires only a finding of internalist lack of epistemic *justification*.

Now one can agree with much of this, yet there remains a serious problem. Take the case of Mary Smith. Suppose that Mary *had* had evidence that her belief that she was being attacked was false (she had been warned on good authority that she would have such hallucinations). But suppose, too, that such was Mary's fear that she panicked—as would (let us suppose) most anyone else suffering such fear—and gave no thought to the warning. In this case, notice that Mary's belief is, from a purely epistemic standard, unjustified, yet it does not appear to render her act culpable. If most anyone else would have given way to such fear, what she did was surely excusable, not culpable. Thus we see that *mere* epistemic unjustifiability of one's belief cannot ground the moral culpability of actions based on those beliefs. The internalist, then, cannot ground Hitler's culpability on the mere epistemic unjustifiability of his beliefs. Even if we concede the unjustifiability of these beliefs from an internalist standpoint, Hitler's actions may remain excusable for all the internalist has shown or maintained.

Or consider a slightly different case. Suppose that a soldier on guard duty shoots one of his own men coming back from patrol.

The soldier did believe that the person coming was an enemy soldier, but had, let us suppose, what the internalist would regard as insufficient reasons to justify this belief. The internalist, let us suppose, insists that the guard may not be responsible for believing this and also insists that the relevant fact in establishing his culpability for the shooting is the guard's lack of justification for this belief (and again not any culpability he has for this belief). But this is most strange. One could understand the claim that the guard is not responsible for his belief itself but instead is responsible for his action insofar as he should have taken some further step or steps to verify this belief before shooting. That, however, is a different view, which we shall consider momentarily. But the claim that it is the lack of justification *itself* that is relevant is most implausible. Suppose, for instance, that the soldier was wired up in such a way that on the mere formation of a relevant belief, his gun would fire. Further verifying actions are now impossible. Would one still insist that even though he is, by hypothesis, not responsible (culpable) for the relevant belief, he is responsible (culpable) for the shooting? Again, this is surely implausible.

3. Action, Responsibility, and Belief

Perhaps it will be allowed, then, that we can be responsible in *some* sense for what we believe.[4] But now, as the previous discussion will have suggested, a philosopher tending to be suspicious of any attempt to expand the scope of direct personal responsibility beyond responsibility for action may offer this caution.

> What you want to call "doxastic responsibility" is really a special case of our responsibility for what we do or fail to do. For what distinguishes Mary from a self-justifying malefactor like Hitler is most relevantly that the exigency of her circumstances left her no time to check, or even to reflect, as to whether her beliefs were true. Hence, we excuse her. And likewise, of course, in the case of the wired-up soldier on guard duty. But the Hitlers of this world have generally had ample time and opportunity to subject their beliefs to reasonable scrutiny. Insofar as they failed to perform the relevant *actions* that would have constituted such scrutiny, they are ultimately to blame for what they did—although not for their beliefs, as such.

This, then, is the view I wish to argue against: the claim that doxastic responsibility is *always* derivative of some more direct responsibility we bear for actions relating to our beliefs (typically actions by way of making sure that they are true). Now of course I do not wish to maintain that this view is wholly mistaken. I do wish to agree that Hitler *is* to blame for failing to take appropriate actions, say, by way of verifying his beliefs before acting on them. My point, however, is this. If we ask—what philosophers generally do not seem to have asked—the further question of why such culpable agents do not perform these appropriate actions, what we find is that underlying this failure on the level of action are still *further* (putatively) justifying beliefs.

Thus, consider what a Hitler might say in response to someone criticizing him for failing to make more of an effort to confirm some of his crucial beliefs before acting on them. Presumably, Hitler would say that he didn't check because he *believed* that he had enough evidence already. (This, after all, is what most of us commonly believe when we do not seek after further evidence.) Moreover, if we tell Hitler that he should have sought additional evidence relative to this last belief, *too* (i.e., tell Hitler that he should have gathered further evidence regarding the belief that no further evidence gathering was required for the original belief), his reply will also be predictable. He will reply that he believed (was disposed to think if suitably queried) that further checking was *also* not required for this belief. Evidently, then, a regress looms here. For any specifiable action failure on the part of the blameworthy believer, it seems quite possible for him to supply a further belief that would have justified that action failure.

Now, to this it may be replied that even if a Hitler may be able to supply a belief to cover each failure at the level of action, the reverse is also true. For in failing to check at the first level (to check on his first-order vicious beliefs [e.g., regarding Jews]), Hitler has *thereby* failed to check at every higher level, has thereby failed to check on whether further checks are necessary, and so forth. Thus it might be thought that the aforementioned regress could be avoided. But there is a reply still to this reply, and I shall put it in this way. What is at issue in such a case is whether one's original assurance that further checks were unnecessary *justified* one's not making further checks. As critics of a Hitler, we want to say that it did not. But why doesn't it? To answer that Hitler is culpable for not conducting checks at level one and thereby failing to conduct checks at every higher level just begs the question of whether that first level failure was justified by Hitler's original assurance.

In many instances, then, if we are to fault an agent for actions founded on beliefs (in relation to which those actions would not be culpable), ultimately we must assign culpability to that agent's relevant beliefs and not to whatever actions he may have taken or omitted taking that led to those beliefs. So I want to say that the difficulty besetting this view is serious. In many instances, agents do not take appropriate actions by way of verifying their beliefs because they believe that such steps are unnecessary. Of course, for these beliefs we may also fault them, but, on pain of generating a vicious regress, we cannot blame them for having these beliefs based on our ultimately faulting them for not taking appropriate actions by way of verifying them.

*   *   *

I have been inveighing against the view that our responsibility for what we believe is derivative, simply, of our responsibility for what we do. Still, this thesis has seemed, and may continue to seem, an attractive option to many philosophers.[5] Let me then try to put my case against it on a stronger footing by more explicitly distinguishing what genuinely *is* a matter of "indirect" or derivative responsibility from what I think is not. To begin, take what is uncontroversially a matter of indirect responsibility, derivative of my responsibility for an action: my responsibility for the intended *effects* of what I do. Suppose that I break a vase by intentionally dropping it; here, we may suppose my culpability for the actual breaking of the vase (an effect of what I did) is indirect, a consequence of my direct culpability for the intentional action of dropping it. Now compare this to a case in which I intentionally bring about a belief by what would normally be an epistemically blameworthy series of actions, say, deliberately taking such steps as I expect will persuade me of the truth of some item and deliberately refraining from those which, I expect, might persuade me of the opposite. Notice that the difference in the latter case is that if I do come to believe this thing is true, my having this belief will be blameworthy only if my enterprise fails to turn up adequate evidence. The culpability of this belief will *not*, then, turn on my original motives for (or intention in) entering into this evidentiary search but instead on what this search generates—by way of giving me *reasons* for my belief.[6] The fact that this search was originally prompted by less than epistemically noble motives does not render my actual formation of it culpable. Now make one final comparison. Suppose that I perform one action with the ignoble goal of creating the motivational backing necessary to get myself to do some act that I know to be morally bad. (For example, I need to motivate myself in order to perform a cruel prank which I must do to pledge a certain fraternity.) Here, too, notice, that if my search for incentives or reasons results in my discovering and doing what is actually the right thing, my moral justification for taking this act is not impaired by the motives that originally prompted my search.

What we see, then, is the following. Even where I do form a belief on the basis of prior, epistemically culpable actions, I am judged as (epistemically) culpable or not for forming the belief independently of this prior action and its motivation (or intention); I am judged, as I am in the fraternity case, on the basis of what reasons (evidence) actually led me to the act (belief). In this respect, both cases are fundamentally different from that of the dropped vase.

I have now completed my replies to each of the strategies that might block the inference I desire: from our responsibility for certain of our actions to our separate and underlying responsibility for certain beliefs. My initial case for doxastic responsibility, however, is not quite complete; I believe it may be strengthened by further considerations, which I offer in the next two sections by way of commentary on some arguments of Richard Feldman and Roderick Chisholm. (However, those who are interested only in the bare-bones argument of this book may move ahead to section 1.6.)

4. Ethics: Subjective and Objective Justification

As Richard Feldman (1985) points out in his useful study of this subject, it is common for writers on ethics to distinguish two notions of ethical justification. One of these corresponds to our notion of what objectively an agent ought to do (i.e., what a correct moral theory or ethical viewpoint would say that she ought to do). The other corresponds to what an agent genuinely and sincerely *thinks* she ought to do. Why do we need both notions? Without commenting on the need for the first, in the case of the subjective notion surely this much may be said. There is an important sense in which a person who has genuinely done her best to determine what course of action is best (i.e., a person who is genuinely *conscientious* in her approach) cannot be blamed for doing what she does.

Now, though, for the main point. As Feldman himself observes, any such notion of "subjective justification" is tenable only if we recognize that mere belief that "I am justified in doing *x*" is not sufficient even for subjective justification. Rather, this belief must itself have some greater positive *epistemic* status than that. What must this positive status be? One natural answer is that the belief that "I am justified in doing *x*" be epistemically *justified*. But this, for reasons we have developed in section 1.2, will not do. If I believe, unjustifiably but in no way culpably, that I ought to do *x*, it hardly seems that *subjectively* it is wrong for me to do *x*. A similar comment, moreover, applies to Feldman's own proposal that subjective justification requires that one have "good reasons" for one's conviction (pp. 407–8). If I lack such reasons, but through no fault of my own, it hardly seems right to call my action *subjectively* unjustified. One may insist, I suppose, on calling it so, yet to what *point* if the agent has genuinely done his best to determine what course of action is right?

The very notion, then, of "subjective moral justification" seems to be built on a notion of doxastic responsibility. This is a subject or a connection (between epistemic virtue and justification) we shall develop at much greater length in chapter 6, sections 6.2–6.3. For now, it suffices to have reinforced, if only slightly, the main conclusion of our previous discussion in this chapter.

5. An Argument of Roderick Chisholm

In his discussion of C. I. Lewis's ethics of belief, Roderick Chisholm (1968, pp. 229ff) offers the following interesting argument for a notion of doxastic responsibility, which both he and Lewis want to defend. Chisholm begins his argument by presenting four premises, each of which, he claims, we are likely to take in isolation to be true, but which, taken all at once, demonstrably leads to a contradiction. I summarize these points as follows.

(i) No act is right unless its consequences are at least as good as those of any alternative act open to its agent at that time.
(ii) An act is right if and only if it is one we may do.
(iii) It is sometimes possible for us to know what we ought and what we ought not to do.
(iv) It is never possible for us to know what all the consequences of an act or possible act will be.

Of course, the contradiction here is that (iv) and (i) will imply that we cannot ever know what act is the right one to do, contradicting (ii) and (iii), which imply that we can. Its solution, according to Chisholm, comes in making a distinction between "right" and "ought" in their absolute sense, which is how he thinks they are to be taken in (i) and (ii), and these terms in their "objective" sense, which is how they are to be taken in (iii) and (iv). What is the difference between these senses? It is simply that an act is objectively right if and only if one has (subjectively) adequate evidence that it is absolutely right (i.e., one is justified in believing that it is absolutely right).

Chisholm concludes as follows:

> Thus we see how all of ethics . . . presupposes the ethics of belief. No act is objectively right unless the agent is *justified* in believing— unless it is *right* that he believe—that the act will have good results. (p. 230)

One comment now on this argument. Inasmuch as an ethics of belief, for Chisholm, involves making belief subject to the same kind of moral assessment as action—with the same basic presuppositions regarding control and responsibility—this argument falls short of its intended target. For all it manages to establish is that the moral evaluation of acts presupposes a notion of "justified belief." What it does not show is that justified belief presupposes any notion of doxastic responsibility.

Now, what Chisholm might have argued is this. We cannot really hold a person culpable for failing to do what absolutely she ought but only for failing to do what objectively she ought. However, if we do hold a person culpable for not doing what objectively she ought, in some cases this will be because of her failure to believe that this was what she ought to do and in other cases this will be because she simply failed to do what she herself believed she ought to do. In the former case, then, and as I have already argued at some length, culpability will require more than an absence of justified belief; it will require a finding of responsibility for the same. Hence, Chisholm's argument, if it is to lead to the kind of full-blown ethics of belief that he himself appears to contemplate, requires, I claim, something like the argument I have offered already in this chapter.

6. Belief and Intellectual Character

It is high time, though, that we resume the main thread of our argument. We had argued, back in section 1.3, that such evil acts as Hitler's were grounded in beliefs for which we must hold him culpable or give up, in large part, any notion of Hitler's moral culpability for his actions. But now it may be suggested that if Hitler's acts were grounded in his beliefs, it is no less true that his beliefs—or at least whatever was culpable about them—were themselves grounded in more basic flaws of intellectual character. Thus, Allan Bullock (1962), one of Hitler's leading biographers and hardly a partisan of any philosophical conception of belief, writes of Hitler's flawed intellectual character:

> Hitler's was a closed mind, violently rejecting any alternative view, refusing to criticize or allow others to criticize his assumptions. He read and listened, not to learn, but to acquire information and find additional support for prejudices and opinions already in his mind. (p. 398)

In short, we have the picture of what must surely count as an epistemically unvirtuous, not to say "vicious," creature; many of those beliefs would surely have been infected by these traits. But all of this, in turn, raises the following difficulty. If the real source of Hitler's culpability lies in his intellectual character, it must lie in something for which he possesses surely no *direct* responsibility. The road from responsibility for action to responsibility for belief now takes a further turn, and what seems in some ways to be a rather unhappy one for the defender of doxastic responsibility. How to prevent responsibility for belief—I must now worry—how to prevent this from dissolving into the mists of time and the murky origins of our "personalities?"

It will be instructive at this point to turn to the first philosopher to systematically address these and many other questions. Now Aristotle does not try to argue that responsibility for belief is derivative of responsibility for one's intellectual character, but he does suggest that responsibility for the latter is derivative of responsibility for action. Thus he speaks of a man whose ignorance results from a lack of due care:

> But perhaps a man is the kind of man not to take care. Still they are themselves by their slack lives responsible for being unjust or self-

indulgent, in the one case by cheating and in the other by spending their time in drinking bouts and the like; for it is activities exercised on particular objects that make the corresponding character. (*N. Eth., Bk. III,* ch. 5, 1114a)

The idea is that this man has become careless mainly by doing careless things. By extension, Hitler has become closed-minded by doing closed-minded things. But does this mean that we can successfully characterize one's culpability at the level of action, rather than belief? No, for what is it to act "closed-mindedly" except to act in ways that exhibit closed-mindedness so far as one's *beliefs* are concerned? Likewise, to use Aristotle's own example, does not carelessness necessarily involve acting in such a frame of mind as not to notice certain relevant things (thus not to form certain relevant beliefs)? Ultimately, then, Aristotle takes us from responsibility for character traits to responsibility for actions productive of those traits and back to responsibility for the beliefs one forms or does not form in the course of those actions.

This last point, however, does not solve our problem. For how do we know that we have avoided a conceptual *circle*? Responsibility for intellectual character may lead us back to responsibility for belief, but how to avoid the suspicion—or more than suspicion—that responsibility for belief leads back to responsibility for epistemic character? In this connection, I think the following distinction is quite helpful. In arguing questions of fault and responsibility—whether these concern the moral or the epistemic sphere—it is important to distinguish what may be termed the relatively "direct" object of responsibility from what might be termed the deeper or ultimate source of blame.

Thus, take the case of a different villain, Iago. Many of this man's actions appear to flow from deep character flaws: tendencies toward malice, resentment, envy, and the like. Yet in the first instance we hold Iago responsible—if for anything at all—for what he *does* and not for these character traits. True, the particular moral quality these actions possess—in Iago's case, their particular immorality—may be said to flow from, and ultimately be caused by the aforementioned nasty personal qualities (and no doubt other nasty ones as well). But this does not mean that his responsibility for his actions is derivative of his responsibility for these character traits, nor even that he is directly responsible for these traits at all. For we will ultimately want to hold Iago responsible not for having these traits, but instead for allowing his conduct to be governed by them.[7]

Apply this analysis now to the case of belief and traits of epistemic character. As with Iago, Hitler's culpability (in regard to his beliefs) may ultimately be traced to those negative traits of intellectual character, such as the aforementioned closed-mindedness, which obviously shape the nature and general direction of his beliefs. But, again, this does not have to mean that Hitler's responsibility for his beliefs is somehow derivative of his more direct responsibility for his closed-mindedness, and so forth. As with Iago, we may want to hold Hitler responsible for allowing these vices to be *exercised* in the formation of his beliefs without holding him responsible in anything like a direct way for the existence of these vices. In this way, we hold Hitler responsible for the doxastic equivalent of conduct—for his use of certain qualities of character—without challenging, what seems a truism, that a person is not directly responsible for, and cannot exert direct control with respect to, character traits themselves. Such, at any rate, is a possibility we shall explore at some considerable length beginning in the next chapter.

Notes

1. Of course, if someone shared *all* of Hitler's beliefs, including his moral convictions regarding the practice in question, this claim becomes trivially true. But, as the discussion to follow will indicate, I am not so much interested in our responsibility for our moral beliefs as in that for the kinds of factual beliefs that typically ground the latter. For instance, it would be quite reasonable to suppose that anyone who shared all of Hitler's *non*moral beliefs would have generally felt justified in acting as he did.

2. See especially section 3.1. Zimmerman, I might point out, goes on to maintain that we are not responsible for our beliefs at all except through our responsibility for willing some action (p. 81).

3. On this notion of an externalist conception (and its rival, internalism), see particularly, William Alston (1986). Two especially influential discussions of the issues here are Goldman (1980) and Bonjour (1980).

4. The arguments presented here may be usefully compared to those of Stevenson (1975) and Plantinga (1983).

Stevenson's approach is similar, to the extent that he grounds doxastic responsibility in the interest society rightfully takes in our having a basic stock—whether in science or elsewhere—of true or well-justified beliefs. Stevenson also rejects, as I do—what seems to me a red herring—the claim that if we hold persons responsible for their beliefs, we will be engaging in some sort of "mind control." As he points out (p. 234), responsibility for belief does not have to imply punishment for false or otherwise misbegotten belief. (As I would conceive this, a person should be punished only for his actions; still, a person's action may be culpable in virtue of their being based on culpable beliefs.)

Stevenson, however, does not really probe the question that mainly interests me here and through much of this study: namely, how this responsibility can be, and why it must be, for belief as opposed to actions that might be expected to affect what we believe.

Plantinga (see pp. 31ff), too, defends the basic doctrine of section 1.2: that moral responsibility for one's action may turn in certain cases on holding a person responsible in some sense for the beliefs that underlie that action. He discusses this with respect to particular, isolated acts like setting an anchor point in descending a treacherous mountain or widespread patterns of belief and action such as those of a Hitler. The basic limitation of Plantinga's discussion, however, is similar to Stevenson's. He raises (p. 31), but does not really attempt to resolve, the question of what our responsibility in such cases consists in, what it depends on. Insofar as Plantinga attempts to answer this question, he suggests that, at least in such cases as Hitler, it may consist in a kind of voluntary choice (p. 36) by which one chooses the path of evil over good. However, any such suggestion amounts to a *rejection* of the notion that moral failure can be grounded in intellectual failure and a corresponding assertion of the reverse dependence.

Plantinga—I might go on to say—is driven to this somewhat desperate measure by what appear to be rather weak arguments. He says, for instance, that an appeal to "carelessness" underlying one's beliefs cannot work in every case as a basis of criticism, for a person might sincerely believe that carelessness, or spontaneity at least, was likely to promote truth (p. 35). Well, first of all, even if that belief is sincere, the point needs to be made that one who holds it is not somehow exempt from the responsibility of exhibiting due care in its formation and retention. This holder, in other words, is not exempt from a careful consideration of potential reasons for rejecting it; a prima facie reason for rejecting it cannot be dismissed on grounds that examination of this case would deviate from "impulsiveness" or "spontaneity." But, notice, then, because such prima facie cases are ubiquitous, it is not altogether clear that such a stance will ever constitute much of a way of avoiding one's conventional intellectual responsibilities.

5. Compare in this regard such writings as the following: Price (1954), Naylor (1985), Clarke (1986), Heil (1983a), Pojman (1986, ch. 13–14), and especially Alston (1988). Perhaps the best example of a normative doxastic theory explicitly framed in terms of a notion of epistemically responsible *action* is Kornblith's (1983), though see also Heil (1983b).

6. This point, it should be noted, is equally valid both for those who

believe and for those who deny that justifiers of a given belief must play some causal role either in its formation or in its sustenance. For, either way, one's justification will be judged according to the evidence one has found. On this contrast, see, for instance, Lehrer (1974, pp. 123–24) and Robert Audi (1983). Either way, the justifiers of the belief will be reasons acquired during the course of one's investigation; and an ill-intended investigation may produce a perfectly justified and responsibly held set of beliefs.

Another point may be noted in this connection. To what I say in here it has been objected that I presuppose a strange or counterintuitive separation of, on one side, the motivation for an act or belief and, on the other, its possible culpability. But I do no such thing. I only separate here culpability for an action or belief from the motivation of a *separate* action or series of actions leading to that action or belief. I do not, however, separate the culpability of a belief or action from the motivation underlying that belief or action itself. On the contrary, insofar as I maintain here that this culpability would depend on one's reason for belief (or action), and insofar as the latter would reflect one's motivation, I maintain that culpability and motivation are very much connected notions.

7. Further argument along these lines is offered in Audi (1991, pp. 309–10).

Chapter Two

Epistemic Virtue

The previous chapter introduced the subject of one's "intellectual character," suggesting that this might hold the key to understanding doxastic responsibility. But what is intellectual character? The composite—it may be answered—of various *traits* of intellectual character (i.e., the various qualities, the virtues and vices, that would comprise such character).[1] But this raises a new question. What is it to be an "epistemic virtue" (or "vice")? (As the title of this chapter suggests, I shall be focusing on virtue, rather than vice, but it will be clear how the vices can be understood as appropriately contrary qualities.[2])

First, a few words of historical background. The general notion of an "intellectual virtue" we inherit from Aristotle. However, Aristotle's approach[3] to these virtues is different from that adopted here.

First, Aristotle distinguishes the intellectual virtues broadly according to the *type* of truth one seeks. Truths he distinguishes as either invariable such as those of science, mathematics, and philosophy, or variable such as those of art and everyday life. However, I make no such initial separation. I am interested in the question of what traits of character are generally conducive to the discovery of truth, irrespective of subject matter. (I am not suggesting, however, that certain traits might not be more applicable to certain subject matters than to others.)

Underlying this difference between our respective investigations, however, is perhaps a more basic one. Aristotle is evidently not interested in (epistemic) character traits as such, not even ones that may be particular to some disciplines but not others. What appears to interest Aristotle, rather, is a more narrowly epistemological project. Having distinguished certain types of knowledge-gaining processes—reasoning, intellectual intuition, and practical wisdom—

he is interested in their respective roles in the attainment of truth (invariable or variable). Aristotle's discussion of intellectual virtue is thus at a piece with his purely epistemological writings, most notably the *Posterior Analytics*. It is not anything like a full analogue of his detailed presentation of the moral virtues as character traits. My own aim, then, is to offer something more like that analogue.

These differences aside, what any contemporary account of epistemic virtue can and should take from Aristotle, at least as its starting point, is his association of the epistemic virtues with *truth*. What I want to suggest, then, as a first approximation, is that the epistemic virtues are those personal qualities (or qualities of character) that are conducive to the discovery of truth and the avoidance of error. Even this small claim, however, raises any number of problems and puzzles, some of the most important of which are as follows.

First, truth-conduciveness may be predicated of all *sorts* of items, ranging from causal processes such as "a good memory" to epistemic principles, rules, and strategies. Now, certainly, the epistemic virtues may be initially distinguished from these other truth-conducive items because the latter are not character traits.[4] But are there, operating at a deeper level, reasons to think that the epistemic virtues should play anything like, as I shall be suggesting, a *special role* in epistemological theory?

Second, there is this familiar, but nonetheless troubling, concern. Let us assume that a Cartesian "evil demon" has, unbeknown to us, made our world such that truth is best attained by thoroughly exemplifying what, on our best crafted accounts, qualify as intellectual *vices*. Presumably, we would not therefore conclude that these apparent vices are and have always been virtues. To be sure, if we were actually to find out that such was the case, *henceforth* we would have to alter our opinions about the worth of these qualities, to start encouraging their development, and so forth. But this is hardly to say that, retrospectively, Galileo should now be regarded as epistemically vicious and, say, Schmalileo, his lazy, intellectually uncurious brother, as epistemically virtuous. At least as I want to conceive them here, the epistemic virtues, and proper judgments respecting them, would not be affected by any such skeptical possibilities. So, for this account, truth-conduciveness cannot, as such, be the distinctive mark of the epistemic virtues. But what connection, then, will there be between truth and epistemic virtue?

Third, if we are to appraise the relative worth or "virtue" of epistemic agents by the truth-conduciveness of their intellectual dispositions, then how are we to accommodate the approximate *equality* of epistemic virtue we find in such diverse agents as Aristotle, Ptolemy, Albertus Magnus, Galileo, Newton, and Einstein? From our current vantage point, we recognize these thinkers as differing greatly in the truth of their respective beliefs and systems of belief, as well as in the truth-conduciveness of their leading ideas and methodological postulates. How can such rough equality in virtue be reconciled with this verific diversity?

Fourth, there is perhaps the most fundamental question of all: whether truth and the avoidance of error offer a complete characterization of the ends of intellectual life. It is at this point, it may be noticed, that my own concerns perhaps touch most closely on Aristotle's. One must concede at least this much to Aristotle: the *mere* holding of many true beliefs and a few false ones is hardly the highest end of intellectual life. To this extent, Aristotle's emphasis on certain specific areas of intellectual life (science, philosophy) as exemplifying intellectual virtue does not seem at all misplaced. It is in such areas that one looks for an explanatory understanding that goes beyond the mere collection, say, of interesting (or uninteresting) truths.

1. Conscientiousness and Virtue

For the time being, we may stay with the familiar twin goals of truth and the avoidance of error, exploring the relation between the motivation to attain these and epistemic virtue. To begin, let us notice that insofar as these are the proper ends of intellectual life, it is perfectly reasonable to suppose that the *desire* to attain these is a prime intellectual or epistemic virtue. In fact, one finds this notion—sometimes under a different name, "epistemic responsibility"—already with some currency in the epistemlogical literature. Hilary Kornblith's (1985) statement here is representative, I think, of this interest:

> We are to measure the epistemic responsibility of agents by the extent to which they are regulated by a desire for the truth. (p. 272)

An "epistemically responsible" person, then, will be *trying* (her best or reasonably hard) to arrive at the truth and to avoid error. And this suggests, certainly, a parallel with moral conscientiousness, with the notion of an agent who is trying her best to do what she thinks is right. In view of this parallel we shall henceforth term such an individual epistemically *conscientious*. Is, though, such conscientiousness sufficient for being (overall) an epistemically virtuous person? No, I will want to say, and for two reasons. First, the twin goals of truth and the avoidance of falsehood are insufficient (as goals for the epistemically virtuous). Second, even if these were sufficient as goals, the mere desire to attain epistemically valuable ends, whatever these may be, is not sufficient to be overall an epistemically virtuous individual.

Let me develop this last point. Notice that just as a moral fanatic may qualify as conscientious without being, on balance, virtuous at all, we can easily imagine an "epistemic fanatic" who is not epistemically virtuous at all (e.g., an extreme dogmatist, absolutely convinced of his possession of the truth, absolutely convinced that his methods of study of some sacred text are every day bringing in powerful new truths). Thus, consider Dickens's characterization of Sir Leicester Dedlock in *Bleak House*:

> [a man] of strict conscience . . . honorable, obstinate, truthful, high-spirited, intensely prejudiced [and] perfectly-unreasonable.

This is the portrait of a conscientious man, and possibly a responsible one in Kornblith's sense, but not, overall, a very virtuous one.[5]

It may be wondered, though, exactly how realistic is this description of the "fanatic." Does the fanatic really love truth, or perhaps lines of Coleridge, cited in Clifford's (1877) "Ethics of Belief":

> He who begins by loving Christianity better than Truth, will proceed by loving his own sect or Church better than Christianity, and end in loving himself better than all. (p. 24)

Are fanatics, once one scratches the surface, found to be in love not with truth, but with themselves and their own pet ideas? Perhaps this is typically the case. But the fanatic I have imagined, unusual as he may be, genuinely does love the truth, and loves his favored doctrine or doctrines out of that primary love for truth. So if, as I assume, this individual falls considerably short of possessing the kinds of personal qualities we would expect of an ideal (or even a reasonably good) truth-seeker, we must acknowledge that such personal qualities extend beyond a mere love or attachment to truth. Again, mere conscientiousness is not enough.

2. Epistemic Virtues: A Preliminary Catalogue

What might be "such qualities in addition to love of truth?" First, let us observe that these qualities, however exactly we are to enumerate them, are not simply additional virtues related to conscientiousness in the way that patience and loyalty may be regarded as distinct and independent moral virtues; rather, these others are forms of conscientiousness—*ways of being conscientious*—related to the latter in roughly the way that moral courage is related to moral conscientiousness. Let me now describe what I take to be the three most important classes of such virtues, then resume discussion of the deeper problem of what makes such qualities epistemic virtues.

First, there are what I will call the virtues of *impartiality*. These include such particular qualities as an openness to the ideas of others, the willingness to exchange ideas with and learn from them, the lack of jealousy and personal bias directed at their ideas, and the lively sense of one's own fallibility. A second class might be termed—with due respect to alleged connection between "vino" and "veritas"—the virtues of *intellectual sobriety*. These are the virtues of the sober-minded inquirer, as opposed to the "enthusiast" who is disposed, out of sheer love of truth, discovery, and the excitement of new and unfamiliar ideas, to embrace what is not really warranted, even relative to the limits of his own evidence.[6] A third I would term the virtues of *intellectual courage*. These include most prominently the willingness to conceive and examine alternatives to popularly held beliefs, perseverance in the face of opposition from others (until one is convinced one is mistaken), and the determination required to see such a project through to completion.

I have deliberately characterized these qualities in quite broad terms. But one may be tempted to adopt a narrower characterization. For example, instead of calling "an openness to others' ideas" a virtue, one might be tempted to speak of the relevant virtue here as "an openness to others' ideas insofar as they are likely to be true," and similarly for the other virtues. Such a change, however, in part for reasons already indicated, introduces too strong a notion of truth-conduciveness into our characterization. (If, unbeknown to all, the words of some crazed oracle turn out to be true, it should not follow that an openness specifically to this person's ideas is an epistemic virtue.) At the other extreme, notice, too, that we may be tempted to think of the actual virtue here as something like "an

openness to others' ideas insofar as one *takes* them to be true."
But this is also a mistake, because it will imply that the most nar-
row-minded dogmatists are actually virtuous. These individuals are
open to those ideas that they *take* to be true. We do not want, then,
to build excessive objectivity or subjectivity into the epistemic
virtues, so I let them stand simply as personality traits, analogous
to such moral personality traits as kindness, rather than to "kindness to those persons who truly deserve kindness" or, its subjective counterpart, "kindness to those persons who one takes to deserve it."

Let me develop these last reflections. How exactly does this
construal avoid the problems of excessive objectivity and
subjectivity? Stay with the example of openness to others' ideas.
Like any other human personality characteristic, openmindedness
is a tendency to respond to certain situations based in part on one's
perceptions or beliefs about that situation. It is not, as such, a
tendency to respond to situations as they are, unmediated by one's
subjective representations. At the same time, like many other
qualities, openness is also be a tendency that affects those very
reactions or perceptions. Thus a patient person is not only patient
relative to her subjective representation of a situation as, say, not
calling for immediate action or judgment; patience must also involve
a tendency to *see* situations in that way (i.e., as not calling for
immediate action or judgment). The same is true, analogously, of
openness. The open-minded person must tend to see others' ideas
as having at least a certain initial plausibility. He or she must be
more than open, relative to what strikes them as initially plausible;
they must have at least some initial tendency to see others' ideas
as plausible.

But if this quality is not to degenerate into mere gullibility, does
not a kind of objective reliability have to be built into this characterization of openmindedness? Must not, in other words, this tendency
somehow be keyed to the *actual* plausibility of others' ideas?

I have basically two problems with any such suggestion. First, it
is not clear that "plausibility" itself is an objective commodity, like,
say, truth. We *find* certain things plausible, but relative to our own
background beliefs. Still, it might be insisted that the openminded
person's reactions are keyed not to some mysterious notion of "objective plausibility," but to the plausibility judgment of some
broader epistemic community (i.e., to "our" judgments as to what
is plausible). Even this, however, seems unpromising. Surely, an
open-minded person—for instance, one coming from some differ-

ent "epistemic community"—might not share our judgments. Second, let us suppose that "plausibility" did denote some purely objective likelihood to be true (however that is to be understood). The mere tendency to have one's reactions, as it were, track such objective likelihoods is not, on reflection, openmindedness at all. It is *sagacity* perhaps; in fact, depending on the type of truth that may be involved, this is a disposition, or family of dispositions, that greatly interested Aristotle (cf. *N. Eth.*, Bk. VI, and the discussion of this in the beginning of this chapter). But, again, it is not openmindedness. For one thing, openmindedness must involve at least some resistance to one's own immediate reactions of unfamiliarity and even implausibility. To this it might be countered that perhaps one's overriding reaction might track objective plausibility even if one's initial reactions did not. But that would, I'm afraid, still miss the point of what openmindedness is: it is the tendency, for example, to resist initial dismissals based on unfamiliarity that partially constitutes openmindedness. Whether it turns out that this resistance tracks, or nearly tracks, objective truth will certainly be of epistemological interest. But it is not part of openmindedness.

Let us consider a new question. What connection do such virtues as openmindedness bear to the underlying virtue of epistemic conscientiousness? Consider, first, intellectual courage (understood as a single generic trait). While it is true that those lacking in intellectual courage are characteristically also lacking in epistemic conscientiousness, these traits are distinguishable. Some persons, for instance, may shun possible sources of contrary ideas to their own, not so much fearing that these ideas are true, as fearing that they lack the wherewithal to avoid being *misled* into thinking them true. Such persons betray a degree of intellectual cowardice but not necessarily any lack of desire for truth. (Again, compare Descartes, HR I, p. 90.) By contrast, the conscientious dogmatist (or "enthusiast") displays an opposite vice: fundamentally he is *over*confident of his intellectual powers, thus unable or unwilling to suspend his doxastic commitments to see whether his certitude is truly warranted.

Let me offer, then, the following suggestion. Fundamentally, the epistemic virtues (besides epistemic conscientiousness itself) are forms by which the latter may be *regulated*. Unregulated by these, bare conscientiousness (as we have seen) may degenerate into some form of intellectual dogmatism, enthusiasm, cowardice, or related evil.[7] That is, bare conscientiousness by no means guarantees a proper orientation toward one's own or others' beliefs, and this is why the qualities we have been enumerating seem so necessary to intellectual inquiry (and integral to our notion of a virtuous inquirer).

3. Epistemic Virtues: Their Epistemic Status

We began by noting that many things—and not just personal qualities akin to the moral virtues—may be termed truth-conducive. And we have now indicated *one* way in which a certain class of apparently truth-conducive qualities stands out as a form of epistemic conscientiousness. In this section I want to explore, in a somewhat more fundamental way, how the *epistemic status* of these qualities may help distinguish them as well from other truth-conducive items.

To begin, an important part of our notion of a virtue, and another legacy of Aristotle, is that these are qualities we want so thoroughly engrained as to be *habits*. We want virtuous acts and the characteristic patterns of motivation underlying them to be exemplified, on appropriate occasions, with much the ease and regularity of habits, and more relevantly here, we want the virtues to be "engrained" in being much more the basis of our actions and evaluation of actions than *themselves* the objects of continuing critical scrutiny and evaluation. This last point is crucial. We would like our children to *be* honest; thus to be disposed to criticize their own and others' dishonesty. But we do not want them now, and only to a limited extent in the future, to be disposed to critically evaluate honesty itself. Nor would we want such critical evaluations of honesty, to the extent that they would be apposite, to emerge from a motivational attitude that is "neutral" between honesty and mendaciousness. Notice, by way of contrast here, that even those of us who regard loyalties to political parties as sometimes a good thing are reluctant to inculcate "loyalty to the Republicans" (or whomever) as a virtue; for this we *want* to be a matter for continuing rational investigation and critical scrutiny. (If there are some who *would* try to engrain "loyalty to the Revolutionary Party" as a virtue, of course all this shows is that unfortunately some people do wish political loyalties to be relatively safe from rational scrutiny.)

Consider now the application of this contrast to the epistemic sphere. A desire to attain the truth is undeniably an epistemic virtue; a desire to uphold, say, an entirely behaviorist psychology would not seem to be one (even if we suppose it to be truth-condu-

cive). Why not? The analogy here with the moral virtues and political loyalties is suggestive. We do not want a commitment to
behaviorism to have the kind of relative immunity from critical
scrutiny that we would accord to a commitment to the truth. Adherence to behaviorism, as much as Republicanism, we think, should
be a matter of continuing reflection, and not in any sense a habit.

Such talk of "inculcating" certain qualities of character, however, raises the question of what *justifies* us in what might seem to
some to be a rather closed-minded and epistemically unvirtuous
practice. Why not leave everything, say, at the level of a "matter
for continuing reflection" and not seek to inculcate any qualities
beyond, say, a love of truth?

I will answer this question in two ways. At a more superficial
level I will point out the extent to which these qualities, precisely
because they do seem to be truth-conducive, are ones that we should
want to inculcate along with a love of truth. Second, at a deeper
level, I will point out—harkening back to our previous discussion
of the need to avoid excessively subjective or objective character-
izations of these virtues—how the particular nature of these qualities requires that, to be effective, they must be more deeply incul-
cated than such attachments as one might have to theories such as
behaviorism or political conservatism.

The first point to be made, then, is that such qualities as openmindedness are widely regarded as truth-conducive. In contrast to
the highly controversial claims of various theories, the truth-
conduciveness of qualities such as openness and intellectual sobriety is widely acknowledged to be a fact, not only by the expert (if
there are "experts" on any such matter as this), but also by the
average nonexpert individual (at least if he or she is suitably queried). Take openness. Unless one starts from the unlikely presumption that one has found the truth already and that the contrary advice and indications of others is liable, therefore, only to lead one
astray, one can hardly possess a sincere love of truth, but no concern about one's own openness. Or, take intellectual sobriety. Here,
too, unless one starts from the unlikely presumption that one's
immediate reactions and unchecked inferences are so highly reliable as not to be improved by any tendency to withhold full assent
until they are further investigated, the virtue of sobriety will have
to be acknowledged. Or, finally, take intellectual courage. Again,
unless one makes an initially unappealing assumption that one's
own ideas—true as they may seem to oneself—are so liable to be
mistaken as to require not only deference to the opinions of others,

but also a deep sense that these are opinions more liable to be correct than one's own (even when one cannot see how or why). Unless one makes such an initial assumption, one will have to acknowledge intellectual courage as a virtue.

Of course, it is possible in each case that an individual might insist on making such an assumption. But consider even our closed-minded fanatic of section 2.1. Even he will recognize, or certainly may be conceived as recognizing, the truth-conduciveness of being open-minded. His problem is not that he entirely disparages openmindedness, for arguably he will not. Basically, his problem (in this regard) will be that he incorrectly believes himself to be (sufficiently) open-minded. He thinks that he is being open-minded, or sufficiently open-minded, when in fact he is not. Likewise, he thinks that he is not precipitous in his judgments, when he is, and so forth. *Must*, though, someone recognize the validity of these qualities of character, on the mere condition that he or she desires truth? Well, if these qualities are readily seen to be truth-conducive, it would be irrational not to want them. It would be as though one wanted to be successful in soldiery, but eschewed all interest in the various qualities (e.g., courage) that are conducive to that end.

In short, then, it does seem that, viewed as general personality traits, apart from their application to any particular situation, these would be truth-conducive and that a person desiring the truth would also desire these qualities. But now two further objections arise, the second on a somewhat more fundamental level than the first.

The first objection is that often we are enmeshed in situations in which it is *not* clear that a particular quality is truth-conducive, or, better, not clear which of two contrary and complementary qualities is more liable to be truth-conducive in that situation. In persisting with a research program is one merely being "headstrong," or is one exhibiting intellectual courage? Likewise, in taking seriously what would seem to be discouraging advice, is one exhibiting a lack of intellectual courage or a desirable openness to the views of others?[8]

Now this objection is troubling to this extent. I want to claim (eventually) that individuals are in many instances *responsible* for being epistemically virtuous, at least to some reasonable degree. So, unlike the externalist discussed in the previous chapter, I cannot be content to argue that these qualities are in fact generally truth-conducive, even though in particular instances we may have hardly a clue as to whether the particular quality or qualities we are exercising are liable to be so. For to the extent that we lack such knowledge, we can hardly be blamed, say, for not being sufficiently virtuous (where this is understood in terms of one's exemplifying the "right" qualities for that situation).

So, again, the objection is potentially an important one. In reply, it will be instructive to look first at a parallel question concerning the moral virtues. Notice that here the same questions arise. In fully punishing an offense, is one being "just" or "merciless?" In not correcting certain deficiencies, is one being "patient" or "lax?" Different moral virtues represent in many instances competing sides of a balanced moral personality, and if we recognize that these qualities have their place in the fully virtuous individual, this does little or nothing to resolve the dilemma of particular cases. The point, though, at least for my purposes, is this. The existence of such difficulties, on one hand, is a reminder of the difficulty of reaching an appropriate balance in any given instance, indeed the impossibility, of a purely general answer to the question of how competing virtues are to be balanced. On the other hand, it is not an argument that constructive efforts in this regard are impossible or that the failure to exert such efforts is excusable. For Einstein not to have persisted in his theoretical researches, say, in 1904, *merely* because these were not supported by the greater share of the physicists of his time would have marked a failure of intellectual courage. For Einstein to have persisted in his research program even after repeated serious experimental setbacks at some point would have constituted a failure in regard to impartiality. These are judgments obviously we can make retrospectively; still, they are based not simply on hindsight but on what would have been knowable at the time.

It is true, then, that the task of weighing competing virtues, whether moral or epistemic, can be a difficult matter. But insofar as one may reasonably attempt to find this balance, and reasonably be judged at least according to one's having made a good faith effort, this difficulty is no final bar to a broadly teleological account of either moral or epistemic virtue.[9] What may appear to raise a more serious difficulty is the skeptical problem mentioned earlier: we have no guarantee that these qualities are, in an absolute sense, truth-conducive *at all*; we have no guarantee that what we take to be epistemic vices may not (unbeknown to us) be virtues. But if that is true, then it may be said that we have no guarantee that our good faith efforts to be virtuous bear any real, objective relation to our goal of attaining truth. For all we know, the more "virtuous" we are, the further we get from the truth.

Still, I would reply, we are able to say this. The epistemic virtues are qualities that a truth-desiring person, given the general conditions that *appear* to obtain in the world, would want to have. Of course, the world could turn out to be a place in which a slavish obedience to some particular authority would be more truth-conducive than the exhibition of any combination of the virtues catalogued earlier. (In fact, the world *is* a place such that some possible individual is such an authority.) But given both the information available to us and its limitations, *these* are the qualities that a truth-desiring person should want to have. Of course, if it were possible to increase radically what we know of the world, perhaps our judgments would change. Perhaps we would discover that slavish obedience to a particular authority was the best route to truth. And, likewise, if it were clearly impossible to know much at all, openmindedness might likewise be inconducive to truth. But given what seems to be the kind of knowledge we are able to possess, these qualities are highly useful. Or perhaps the point is best put in this way. Absent a guarantee of how the world is, a truth-desiring person can do no better than to rely on the way it appears to be and, thus, the general sorts and general limitations of knowledge that we appear to possess. It is admittedly relative to such broad judgments that the qualities we have singled out turn out to be virtues, but one can hardly hope to avoid all such judgments. Recall that even our epistemic fanatic is not so far from sharing our judgments of how the world is that he will not recognize, at least in principle, the truth-conduciveness of these qualities.

Let us summarize the main lines of the discussion so far. We have observed that our notion of an epistemically virtuous individual appears to include, in addition to a simple desire to attain truth and avoid falsehood, certain collateral virtues that we then went on to catalogue. These virtues are distinguished, first as qualities that we would be desirous of inculcating as habits of thought and action, as opposed to mere principles currently taken to be true but entirely open to later revision or outright rejection. Challenged to justify this entrenchment, we have responded by pointing out the extent to which these are qualities that most anyone, possessed simply of a desire for truth, would want to have regardless of the uncertainties surrounding their relative desirability in particular cases. Now I turn to what I regard as the second and more fundamental reason justifying this entrenchment.

Return to our previous discussion of the epistemic virtues as neither excessively objective nor subjective in their basic constitu-

tion, of, for example, openmindedness as an openness keyed neither to objective fact nor simply to one's own opinion as to objective fact. And consider once again the example of kindness. Notice
that the mere acquisition of certain relevant *beliefs* concerning what
kindness is and concerning the fact that one ought to be kind will
hardly be enough to make one kind. It may be enough to render
one disposed to act—or, better to try to act—kindly whenever one
believes one ought to be kind, but this, again, is an excessively
subjective rendering of the virtue of kindness. And the same clearly
is true of such traits as openness. Learning that "one ought to be
open" is not enough to render one an open person. To the extent
that this is impartible at all, its being imparted requires a more
fundamental alteration of one's underlying dispositions to respond
to others. One must, as indicated earlier, tend not only to respond
affirmatively to ideas one finds plausible, but also tend (to some
extent) to find certain unfamiliar ideas at least initially so—at least
initially worthy of interest and further consideration. The mere
belief that one ought to be open-minded is insufficient for this, and,
likewise, for the other broad classes of virtues catalogued earlier.

Thus there is a second and arguably more fundamental reason
for treating the epistemic virtues as different from other merely
truth-conducive strategies, principles, theories, and the like. For
them to be effective as virtues, they cannot be imparted merely as
beliefs but require instead a more fundamental attachment. But it
is just this kind of deep, underlying, and—some will say—basically *irrational* attachment that is worrisome in the present connection. Some will object at this point that, on this construal, the
epistemically virtuous person threatens to become a mere "creature of habit,"[10] a mere automaton who can hardly be responsible
for his virtuous (or less than virtuous) activities. Others may perhaps raise this more technical formulation, drawing on Aristotle.
The *moral* virtues are, at least in certain salient instances, exer-
cises of will.[11] Insofar, then, as these virtues are also to be described
as "habits" this is because they are tendencies prompting one toward some act of will, or "choice" to use the Aristotelian term. To
that extent, they are dispositions of a highly rational sort; for choice,
as Aristotle will correctly insist, is at least in its most central instances a highly rational activity. But can we say analogously that
the *epistemic* virtues, as you characterize them, are habits in anything like this rational sense?

In reply, I should first beg leave to give a fuller consideration of
these matters in the next chapter, in the context of my discussion

there of the crucial topic of our *responsibility* for exercising the various epistemic virtues. Here, though, a few points may still be made. First, of course it may be said that not all habits are "mindless habits" or anything of the sort; so there is no reason to equate the virtuous person with anything like a mindless creature. One can habitually tie one's shoes, but one can also habitually relate things people say to propositions of Spinoza, certainly not a mindless, if not always a useful, activity. Second, on the account that I shall be proposing, the epistemic virtues are dispositions if not governing choice, at least affecting the will. For they will be, in part, dispositions to put forth an appropriate *effort*. They are not dispositions to will or choose particular beliefs or systems of belief. They are, however, dispositions to exert oneself by way of making sure, for example, that one has examined all of the relevant evidence, that one is not being closed to new ideas, and so forth. These are all *active* frames of mine; they are not the dull, automatic responses of a mere "unthinking" habit.

Before moving on to consider the different question of what other ends (besides truth and the avoidance of error) the epistemic virtues may be considered as directed at, let us review where we stand in relation to some of the theoretical concerns enumerated at the start of this chapter.

First, we asked there what, beyond the obvious point that the epistemic virtues are to be conceived as character traits, might distinguish these from other truth-conducive items. This we have tried to answer in terms of the special entrenchment one wants, and should want, these virtues to have. As to whether these virtues ought to play any special role in epistemological *theory*, I postpone discussion of this until the last chapter (in which the topic of virtue and epistemic justification is taken up).

Second, we raised the concern over the possibility of a skeptical contretemps by means of which truth is best served by what we currently regard as epistemic vices. The intuition that this ought not to change our estimation of these as genuine vices is accommodated by our account, insofar as the virtues are not necessarily truth-conducive in an absolute sense. They are simply qualities that a truth-desiring person would want to have, given certain broad features of what we take ourselves to know and not know about the way the world is.

Third, we raised the question of the relative equality holding of such diverse inquirers as Aristotle, Aquinas, and Einstein. This, too, is readily accommodated by our underlying conception of epistemic virtue, for we can agree that these thinkers were roughly equal in the qualities we have distinguished as epistemic virtues, even as they differed greatly in the truth or truth-conduciveness of their leading ideas, intellectual methods, and the like.

4. The Goals of Epistemic Life

Finally, I turn to the last of the four questions, or difficulties, posed at the outset—whether truth and the avoidance of error were rich enough desires for the epistemically virtuous. Here I want to spell out briefly my conviction that these desires are *not* rich enough for the virtuous, but also show why this discovery has little (if any) bearing on my larger project.

The case that truth is not enough for the truly intellectually virtuous—at least the ideally virtuous—is fairly straightforward. The larger goals of epistemic life cannot be confined to the mere acquisition of truths, let alone the mere acquisition of truths already known to others in the intellectual community. For, ideally, one seeks not only truth but *science*. That is, one seeks a kind of deep, economical, explanatory understanding of the world and ourselves as part of the world. One seeks to participate somehow in the advance of this understanding—if not by directly contributing to it, by somehow indirectly assisting it or perhaps just by becoming knowledgeable of its results. I take it as obvious that this goal, or these goals, cannot be defined simply in terms of learning *many* truths (or many truths and few falsehoods).

This having been acknowledged, however, we must ask what additional personal traits (if any) are required for the achievement of these goals. My answer would be this. Certainly, if our goals have broadened, we must suppose that the intellectually virtuous person's *desires* must be broadened correspondingly. She will seek more than truth and the avoidance of error; ideally, she will seek these other goals as well. Beyond this obvious need to expand one's goals, however, it is not clear that any different set of "regulative" traits are now required—beyond impartiality, intellectual courage, and the like. For these traits are obviously broad enough to characterize not only epistemically virtuous activities on a small "everyday" scale, but also those in science as well. Successful science depends, rather, on intellectual *capacities* beyond those typically exemplified in, or required by, more ordinary situations in life. But such qualities—for example, the mathematical brilliance or ex-

perimental innovativeness of the great scientists—are not what I
have wished to class as epistemic virtues.

Here, however, it will help to pull together not only this discussion, but also a great deal in this and succeeding chapters if I explain my motivations here.

5. Virtues and Capacities: Motivations of the View to Be Developed

I have not tried in this chapter to *define* in a strict sense my notion
of epistemic virtue. Instead, I have begun basically with a rough
idea of these as truth-conducive personality traits, analogous to such
morally significant personality traits as patience, loyalty, and benevolence. Then I have sought to enumerate them, point out their
interrelation, and provide an account of the basis of "entrenchment."
As traits of intellectual *personality*, these qualities differ from such
truth-conducive qualities as, say, mathematical genius. The latter
is an intellectual capacity, rather than a personality trait. But why
worry about this difference? Why not broaden our concept of epistemic virtue to include both?

My answer relates the deepest motivations underlying my view.
I want to use the notion of an epistemic virtue to give an account—
an account that I have already gone some way toward arguing that
we need—of doxastic *responsibility*, of responsibility for belief. To
this extent, I will be interested in those qualities of intellectual
character whose exercise is subject to our control. Correspondingly,
I will be interested in those qualities of character for whose exercise or nonexercise we can properly be blamed or credited. Whatever their relevance for epistemology, capacities like mathematical
genius (or even just simple "creativity") fall into a different category in this regard).[12]

Notes

   1. Must every quality of intellectual character be a virtue or a vice?
I see no problem in saying so if we also allow that a quality like aggressiveness may be a virtue in certain situations and a vice in others. This,
however, is not a complication I shall pursue.
   2. This chapter began life as a revision of my previous work (1987a),
but has since taken on more or less a life of its own. It also draws, though
to even a lesser extent, on other work of mine (1985, 1987c).

3. On Aristotle's account of intellectual virtue, see the *Nichomachean Ethics*, Book VI. The discussion below is obviously not an attempt to summarize the whole of Aristotle's views but merely to highlight certain differences between his approach and my own.

4. I do not follow, then, the unrestricted kind of teleological approach of Ernest Sosa (1985, 1991), wherein any truth-conducive capacity, regardless of whether it is a personal quality, counts as an epistemic virtue.

5. James Wallace (1978, p. 93) cites these lines as illustrating the correlative thesis that *moral* conscientiousness does not suffice for (overall) moral virtue. A useful discussion of conscientious but unvirtuous agents may be found in Lorraine Code (1983). Richard Foley (1987) offers an account of "epistemic rationality" in which the well-entrenched beliefs of such an intellectual fanatic might count as epistemically rational, as these would be ones that, presumably, this individual would continue to hold on reflection. This, for me, disqualifies Foley's theory as a conception of epistemic virtue. For further critical discussion of Foley's view, see, for instance, Moser (1989).

6. Intellectual sobriety thus requires an absence of what Descartes in the *Discourse on Method* terms "precipitation"; likewise, impartiality will require an absence of what he terms "prejudice." References to Descartes will henceforth be to the Haldane and Ross translation of his writings, indicated by "HR" plus volume and page number: here HR I, p. 92. See also in this regard the commentary by Gilson (1947) on this passage (pp. 198–99). Two pages earlier Descartes, in effect, distinguishes the excessively bold nature from what I call, just below in the text, the "intellectual coward."

7. A correlative point is that when these regulative qualities are not exemplified out of an underlying conscientiousness, they do not constitute an exhibition of epistemic virtue. To listen patiently to others' ideas merely to curry favor with them, and not out of any interest in learning something from them, is obviously not to exemplify any epistemic virtue.

8. Hilary Kornblith raised basically this objection against a (very much shorter) version of this chapter read at the Eastern Division Meeting of the American Philosophical Association, December 1986.

9. Consideration may be given here to the following. Assuming that there is a ideally correct balance of qualities (whether drawn from our catalogue of virtues or not), why can we not say that the ideally virtuous person is simply the one who exemplifies this balance regardless even of whether she knows that she does? The problem here obviously is one of knowledge. As the previous objection insists, we do not know what this balance is. Thus, any difference between the qualities exemplified by this hypothetical virtuous individual and someone who was simply trying his reasonable best to exemplify the qualities that seemed to him to be most likely to yield epistemically desirable ends in that situation would be entirely fortuitous. The hypothetical virtuous individual, in other words,

would *not* have a more virtuous underlying motivation than the person just doing his reasonable best. Hence, by the argument of note 7, the hypothetical individual would not, on reflection, count as any more virtuous the other. At *best*, the hypothetical individual would count as equally virtuous (assuming her motivation was equally truth-oriented). This view, then, avoids the problem that besets the externalist or reliabilist views alluded to in chapter 1: namely, that in any given case, a true belief (however fortuitously it may appear to have been arrived at) will have been arrived at by a method that was reliable at least for that particular situation. See, for example, the discussion of this in Conee and Feldman (1985) and Kvanvig (1986).

10.   Compare in this regard Von Wright (1963, p. 143) and Hunt (1978, pp. 178–79). Of course, Aristotle himself saw no conflict between a notion of the virtues as proper habits and the exercise of virtue as under one's voluntary control: Both notions are contained in the Aristotelian dictum, mentioned a bit later in the text, that virtue is a disposition concerned with *choice* (*N. Eth.* 1107b).

11.   Compare Aquinas on this point, *Summa Theologica*, 1a2ae, 57, 1. Saint Thomas is recognizing here that the intellectual virtues cannot be mere tendencies toward intellectual activity nor capacities to engage in such activity but must in some sense be directive of the will. Because he denies that intellectual virtue is concerned with our outer behavior, he settles on the notion that these virtues govern our determination to engage in an interior act, a "study of the truth." Aquinas here struggles valiantly to find a respect in which there can be intellectual virtues, given that the intellect (on his own view and, of course, Aristotle's) is not responsible for conduct. Aquinas settles (57, 1) on the notion that there can be both habits bearing on outer conduct and habits bearing on inner conduct (in particular, on the study of the truth). On the limitations of any thesis that virtue is an expression always of will, see Roberts (1984).

12.   Some further comments are apposite here on the detailed and complex view of the epistemic virtues advanced by Kvanvig (1992). Like Sosa (see note 4), Kvanvig begins with a quite broad characterization of the epistemic virtues as embracing any truth-conducive personal characteristic—including both what I would call traits of intellectual personality and mere "capacities" (see esp. p. 8). I have already indicated in the preface my reasons for not favoring such an approach.

A further difficulty I have with Kvanvig's initial construal is that he rather indiscriminately groups such qualities as "openmindedness" and "creativity" as epistemic virtues—treating all of these as epistemic motivations that, at least for the virtue epistemologist, are adequate substitutes for a more deontological emphasis on a truth-oriented motivation (p. 6). As the account proposed in this chapter attempts to bring out, however, the epistemic virtues are anything but surrogates for a truth-oriented motivation. Where they do not coincide with the latter, they are forms by which the latter is to be regulated. (Here it seems to me that Kvanvig is simply thrown off the track by following the analogy of "virtue ethics" as an alternative to a strict Kantian regard for moral rightness.) This point notwithstanding, however, one still wishes to treat qualities like creativity differently from, say, openmindedness. The latter is evidently a form of conscientiousness in the sense that "openmindedness" is properly an openness to possible *truths* emanating from others. Creativity, by contrast, is not per se a truth-related quality at all. I would prefer, for my part, to treat it as a capacity somewhat on a par with, say, mathematical genius (cf. the discussion of this in section 2.4).

Kvanvig's failure to take full account of the difference between truth-conducive capacities like creativity and virtues in a narrower sense leads him into further difficulties, it seems to me, later in his study. For later (pp. 116ff) he will raise, what seems to be a false problem, of someone for whom wishful thinking is truth-conducive. Not wanting to count such wishful thinking as a virtue, he begins a gradual process of amending the proposed end to which the epistemic virtues are conducive. Now, strictly, it seems to me, Kvanvig positively *ought* to regard such wishful thinking as a virtue because it is quite on a par with other capacities (like an extraordinary memory) which he has no problem counting as virtues. For my part, such fortuitous wishful thinking (assuming that one is not able to know when it is and when it is not occurring, and I don't see how one could know this if it is truly wishful thinking) is not an epistemic virtue, because it is does not involve a direct regard for truth, nor is it a means by which one could regulate such a regard for truth. It would simply be an unusual truth-conducive capacity, not different in kind from visual acuity.

Chapter Three

Epistemic Virtue and Responsibility I

We have characterized the epistemic virtues as qualities of character. But how or in what way are we responsible for the exercise of these in the formation and retention of our beliefs? That will be the central question facing us here, in the next chapter, and often in the following chapters.

1. Sketch of a Theory

First, we will need to go back to the discussion of Iago and Hitler in section 1.6. Recall the point there was that persons can be responsible—and in what seems to be a direct way—for the exercise of certain qualities of character (qualities like Iago's malice), even as they bear nothing like the same kind of responsibility for the existence or origination of these qualities. Now to set the stage for a comparable discussion of our responsibilities for our epistemic character traits and their exercise, we need to frame a more definite conception of the exercise of *moral* virtues (and vices) and the nature of our responsibility for these. In this regard, I would want to distinguish a number of ways by which we can be responsible in what appears to be a direct way for the exercise of these character traits.[1]

First, and most obviously, a person may simply try to be patient, courageous, kindly, and so on. These are qualities, in other words, one can exercise by trying to exercise them. In the case of moral vices, though, can a person try in the same way to be cruel, impatient, or cowardly? Although the motivational pattern in such cases might be more difficult to understand, certainly this can and often does happen: Villains try to be cruel, gluttons revel in their own gluttony, and so forth.

What is much more common, though, especially in the case of the vices, is psychologically a rather less direct mode of exercise. In this case, one tries to accomplish something else and thereby exemplifies, or allows oneself to exemplify, the character trait in question. For example, by acting in pursuit of more specific motives and concerns, Iago allows his conduct to exemplify the quality of being malicious. In giving vent to his desire to throw an eraser at an unresponsive student, a teacher may thereby allow himself to exercise impatience. Nor is such determination limited to vices. A person may succeed in exercising morally *good* qualities by trying to accomplish all sorts of ends ranging from the particular ("I want to help that person") to the very abstract ("I want to do what is right").

Now, in each case it is possible to draw analogies on the side of the epistemic virtues.

First, quite obviously, people can and do try to exemplify these qualities. In hearing another's argument, I may try to be impartial, or, if I know that I am prone to being unduly influenced by others (say, because I am too quick to accept the validity of considerations emanating from perspectives other than my own), I may try to be courageous enough to stick to my initial viewpoint. Again, one may need to try to avoid wishful thinking or "rushing to judgment," especially if she recognizes herself as prone to these vices.

In addition, a person may, especially in the case of vices, allow himself to fall victim to these without trying to exemplify them. Thus, even though there are problems with describing Hitler as deliberately closed-minded or prejudiced (if he is aware that he is being prejudiced or closed-minded, his vice becomes one of *morality* rather than cognition), Hitler can *allow* himself to be closed-minded by failing to be adequately concerned with the truth of his beliefs. (My comments here anticipate the more extensive discussions of epistemic negligence and unconscious epistemic vices at sections 4.2–4.3.) To be sure, under such circumstances, Hitler probably would want to deny that he is being closed-minded—or certainly that he is being unduly so—but that is hardly a matter in relation to which he can claim infallibility. And if he is, despite his protestations, being closed-minded, it may also be true that he is allowing himself to be closed-minded. (Likewise, Iago may deny that he is being malicious.) Moreover, as in the case of the moral virtues, one may be responsible for the exercise of epistemic virtues, as well as vices, because one is trying to accomplish some related end. For example, a person may be trying simply to arrive at the truth or to follow the relevant evidence but in so doing, succeed also in being intellectually courageous, open-minded, or judicious. Nor need a person's goals be explicitly framed so abstractly. One may also exemplify such virtues in the course, say, of trying "to solve this problem" or to "figure out why such and such a substance is being emitted." In short, the cases of the moral and epistemic virtues seem comparable in this regard: Their exercise may be controlled at three levels: directly trying to exemplify them, trying to exemplify some overarching moral or epistemic characteristic (such as doing one's duty or arriving at the truth), or explicitly trying to accomplish only some relatively specific task.

Let us carry this analysis one step further. In looking at these three levels of trying in relation to our conception of the epistemic virtues, one comment seems especially pertinent. The first level corresponds to the various "regulative virtues" distinguished in section 2.3. The second level, at which one is trying "to arrive at the truth" or perhaps "to be guided by the evidence," basically corresponds to the overarching virtue of conscientiousness (although there is a complication here that I shall discuss to momentarily). The third, however, at which one is trying, say, merely to accomplish some particular task like "determining whether 457 is a prime number," corresponds to no particular virtue at all. Is that a problem? No, or it is only at the most superficial level of analysis. Obviously, if one is exemplifying such a virtue as "care" in the process of working out such a problem, one must be trying not simply to solve this problem but to solve it *correctly*, thus to arrive at the truth concerning this matter.

This last consideration allows us to make a helpful simplification: We can now say that individuals are responsible for the exercise of epistemic virtues either by trying to exemplify some particular ("regulative") virtue or by trying—even though one may have other goals as well and even though one's goals will not have to be framed in just these terms—to be epistemically conscientious. Likewise, we can say—in the case of our responsibility for the exercise of corresponding vices—that even if we do not deliberately exemplify these, we may certainly be responsible for these insofar as we have not tried sufficiently hard to exemplify some virtue (especially that of conscientiousness).

But I now turn to the problem alluded to earlier, which involves the difference between pursuing truth and being strictly guided by one's evidence. An example will help bring out this difference.

2. Deontology, Consequentialism, and Epistemic Virtue

The case is this (cf. Firth [1981]). Mary Curry is a famous scientist who has just been told on good authority that she is dying of cancer. Even in her despondency, she realizes that if she could only get herself to believe that she has a good chance to recover, regardless of whether this would materially affect her actual chances of recovery, this would enable her to complete in her remaining months the important research in which she has been engaged, thus accomplishing her ultimate goals of discovering truth and extending knowledge.[2] Now the first question to ask about such a case is whether, as an epistemically virtuous person, Mary should believe, or try to believe, this proposition (that she will recover).

Now, in general, it is certainly correct to say that an epistemically virtuous person is a truth-seeker (as well as a knowledge and understanding seeker); it is also correct to say that an epistemically virtuous person is someone who strives to be "guided by the evidence" (and not by evidentially irrelevant considerations). Here, however, these goals appear to conflict. To be sure, there is no conflict between Mary's trying to be guided by the evidence and Mary's trying to arrive at the truth concerning this one proposition ("that I shall recover"); but there is certainly a conflict between these goals—or really this single goal—and the longer-termed *maximization* strategy of promoting truth, knowledge, and other epistemically desirable ends. (Compare in this regard the discussion of these ends in section 2.4.)

The question in this case is whether one should exercise epistemic virtue in accordance with simple conscientiousness ("trying one's best to see whether this proposition is true") or, in preference to this, in accordance with some strategy of maximizing certain desirable epistemic ends. The latter, notice, constitutes a fairly precise analogue of what would be a "consequentialist" program in ethics whereby one aims to maximize some good, such as pleasure or knowledge, even if this must be accomplished by means of some otherwise impermissible action. (Here of course the otherwise impermissible act is accepting as true what has patently inadequate evidentiary support.) Is Mary, then, to be guided by the relevant evidence concerning this one proposition, or is she to be guided by the longer-termed considerations of gaining many more truths? Should Mary be the epistemic equivalent of a "deontologist" in ethics—strictly bound to the virtuous formation of this one belief—or should she instead believe in accordance with what will apparently bring about the best epistemic consequences in the long run? Let me address this question in two parts.

(a) Mary cannot—she could not even if she were *not* an epistemically virtuous person (see the discussion of the "Bubba Case" in section 5.2)—simply direct her beliefs to go contrary to the perceived direction of the evidence. Mary recognizes that the evidence points (let us say) decisively in the direction of her nonrecovery; to this extent, she places at least some considerable *credence* in this. Given this, it seems that she cannot, whether she wishes to or not, just by a single act of will disregard (i.e., *succeed* in disregarding) her own appreciation of this evidence and boldly arrive in one fell swoop at the notion that she will recover.

(b) At the same time, Mary remains free to resolve to take such steps as she may think will serve to *bring about* over time in herself a conviction that she will recover. Despite the fact that she cannot now simply accept her recovery as a fact (or even a probability), Mary may view her future acceptance of this recovery as a good, even mandatory thing for her to believe. And she may, of course, resolve to carry out and begin to carry out steps designed to secure this desired conviction.

I shall have more to say about the (b) situation momentarily, but first let me underline an important implication of the discussion under (a). Insofar as epistemic virtue is to be exercised directly in the formation or retention of a given belief, such virtue must be exercised in accordance with whatever reasons one has for thinking that *this belief would be true*. Other reasons, even those relating to the long-term interests of truth and knowledge, as we have seen, are at most relevant to the doxastically *indirect* exercise of epistemic virtue (i.e., relevant at the level of deciding what actions to take by way of bringing about some desired belief state).[3]

Returning now to the case of (b), the question remains as to what an epistemically virtuous person should do under these circumstances. Should Mary endeavor simply to accept the evidence or should she perhaps labor mightily against this and try to believe the opposite for the good of science?[4] Let me suggest at least a partial answer to this question. I do not think it would be appropriate for an epistemically virtuous person to endorse an *unqualified* consequentialist position according to which one may, or should, always believe what would serve the long-term interests of knowledge. Any such policy, and any such habit or tendency (were this policy to be so engrained), would clearly be highly dangerous.

Arguably, it would fail even by consequentialist standards; for arguably it would lead individuals to disregard evidence when this action did *not* ultimately serve the long-term interests of truth. Thus an epistemically virtuous person will not want to be guided by maximizing considerations. But it would be permissible in this situation for Mary to be guided by a more *restricted* consequentialism. Owing to the exceptional character of these circumstances, Mary can hardly be understood as endorsing an unrestricted consequentialism if she embarks on a policy of trying to get herself to believe that she will recover. At most, she can sensibly be understood as endorsing a view that under *exceptional* circumstances considerations of evidence may be overridden in the interests of the long-term extension of knowledge. And such a concern can hardly be inconsistent with the broader idea of an epistemically virtuous person. Notice, though, it would *also* be consistent with this broad idea if Mary were to reject any thought of convincing herself that she would recover. That would be an extreme stance, to be sure, but not one that would somehow impugn her epistemic virtue. On the contrary, some might take such a rejection as a fitting culmination to a life dedicated to the maintenance of certain standards of truth and evidence. In short, the bare idea of an epistemically virtuous person is broad enough in such instances to embrace either a strict deontological approach or a less strict, qualified consequentialism.

3. Direct Doxastic Responsibility

Let us return to our main discussion. Before launching on the topic of Mary Curry and her possible inclinations toward either a consequentialist or deontological approach to the advancement of knowledge, we explained certain ways in which an individual can be regarded as responsible for the exercise of qualities of character (moral or epistemic) basically, by trying either directly or indirectly to exemplify these. But how do we effect a transition from such responsibility at the level of qualities of character to anything like a direct responsibility for whatever *beliefs* (or abstaining from belief) may result from the exercise of these?

Let me set up my discussion by giving voice to some of the doubts that a critic may already have at this point:

> One may readily allow that we are *indirectly* responsible for beliefs; and I am willing to allow that one way in which this

indirect control can be achieved is through mental actions of one sort or another (e.g., by acts of concentrating on what one wants to believe or on the evidence that may exist for what one wants to believe); (cf. Price [1954], 17ff). I take it, then, that any control one exerts with respect to her exemplifying this or that epistemic virtue would be an instance of such control. Persons may, for instance, gird themselves not to be gullible, to pay closer attention, or the like. And all of this, insofar as it may in turn affect what she believes, will qualify as indirect control. But I reject outright any suggestion that such control might be direct.

How do I reply to such a point? First, it is important to distinguish the attempt to do something that is aimed at causing oneself to have or not have a certain belief—to distinguish this from what would serve as a *modality* of the belief-forming process (i.e., as a way of forming or avoiding forming a given belief in a given situation). Thus, deliberately deciding to focus one's attention on the evidence favoring one side of a particular question is an attempt to indirectly alter one's beliefs (i.e., to cause oneself to have a belief that one does not presently have but wishes to have). But forming a belief with care (e.g., care that one not be precipitous in one's judgment or that one not reject emotionally unpleasant facts) is not the same thing. In trying to form one's belief carefully, one is not doing or trying to do something that will cause one to have any particular belief.

To reinforce this notion, however, it is helpful to consider the following analogy. Take the case of a man who is carving wood carefully. Notice, first, that carving wood carefully differs importantly from such things as carving wood "nervously." He is able to *apply* care to the carving of the wood; it is a modality of his action that he controls. By contrast, although "nervousness" is like "care" in describing a state of mind, it is simply a state of mind one might have in acting; it is not something one applies to an action and not a mode with respect to which one is in control of one's action. Thus, whereas the man can comply with the request to "carve the wood carefully," "carve the wood nervously" can only be complied with by something like waiting until he becomes nervous or making himself nervous, then carving as long as the nervousness lasts. Carefulness, thus, is an inner state but one whose outer expression is subject to one's control in a way in which such inner states as nervousness is not.

There is a related point—and, for my purposes, ultimately more important point—to be made in this connection. If carving wood carefully is not a matter of doing something when a certain inner state happens to come over one, neither is it making sure *only* that one is in a certain inner state. Thus it would not be correct to describe our carver as in direct control of his frame of mind, but only as in indirect control of whether his overt acts are careful, as though what he did was to ensure a certain kind of pure inner state of carefulness that, independently of any further care on his part, issued mechanically in careful acts. What we should say, rather, is that his control of his frame of mind and his control of the expression of that frame of mind in action are at a piece. Being careful, or taking care, is a mental state subject to one's direct control; but such control, or the exertion of such control, is not a separable action by means of which one brings about careful movements of one's limbs. Rather, there is a single application of mental effort that may be variously described from a more inward standpoint as, say, "maintaining one's concentration" or from a more outward-looking standpoint as, say, "moving one's fingers in a careful way."

Where does this leave us in the case of belief? It seems that there may be a problem in this case. In the case of overt action, we were readily able to distinguish the inner state of being careful and its outer expression in carving wood. But does *belief* involve anything like this duality? My answer is that, properly understood, belief certainly does. Notice that just as the carver's maintenance of due care did not consist simply in the maintenance of a given inner state that more or less automatically translated itself into careful movements, care in what one accepts as true likewise is not a matter simply of maintaining an attitude that more or less automatically translates itself into carefully formed beliefs. No, in both cases, care involves the maintenance of an appropriate frame of mind that is to be *expressed* as one confronts the medium in question. The difference is simply that in the one case the "medium" is what the carver is working on, in the other it is what propositions the subject is confronted with and which he or she must either accept or not. Just as the carver's care is expressed *in* his work, the believer's care is expressed in the attitude (the care) she actually uses, or fails to use, in the process of evaluating and ultimately accepting or not accepting the propositions in question. Just as the carver can display care in the actual process of his work, the believer can only do so in the actual process of deciding what to believe given certain evidence. There is no such thing as just "being in a careful frame of mind," in the absence of any matters, physical or intellectual, for one's actual consideration.

Let us now broaden our notion of care to embrace the full range of epistemic virtues. How can we do this and why are we entitled to do it? My answer is this. "Care," as the generic term for what our carver is exerting, really embraces many more specific concerns. Thus the carver may be taking care specifically that his knife does not slip, or that he doesn't press too hard, and so forth. But whichever of these more specific concerns he has, it will remain true that "care" represents a modality of his carving and not some prior action. Likewise, then, insofar as the epistemic virtues can be readily seen as ways of exerting forms of care (e.g., care that one not believe precipitously, care that one remain open-minded, etc.) any of them may, under appropriate circumstances, be understood as modalities of the belief-forming process. One's mental "set" may differ, and may be expected to differ, from situation to situation. One will not be expected to exert care simultaneously with respect to all of these virtues. But that is not what I wish to claim or need to claim. My point is only that a notion of generalized "epistemic care" will have some more specific embodiment in any given case.

There is one more point to be made in this connection. In denying that one's doxastic responsibility is typically indirect, one is *not* denying that it is incomplete. My thesis, simply put, is that doxastic responsibility is typically direct and *in*complete. Doxastic responsibility, I want to say, is grounded in the control we have with respect to one aspect, one modality, of the belief-forming or belief-holding process. With respect to other aspects, then, there is no claim to direct or even indirect control. More importantly, there is no claim here that the *existence* (or occurrence) of a given belief is itself subject to one's control. In a given case I may be unable to control whether I hold a given belief, even if it is within my power whether I believe this item *virtuously* or not.

This last point, however, raises what may seem a troubling question. Suppose that S believes that p unvirtuously; suppose, too, that S could have been virtuous under these circumstances, but that S would still have believed p. Less abstractly, suppose that Hitler, say, would still have held many of his vicious beliefs even had he been as epistemically virtuous as he was capable of being. In that case, whereas we can still fault him for a lack of virtuous efforts, it seems that we cannot truly blame him for these beliefs themselves, hence, at least by the argument of chapter 1, for many of the actions he took on the basis of these beliefs. Would this not, then, unseat much of what I have tried to accomplish heretofore in this study? Have we not allowed moral responsibility for action— in the very cases in which I want to account for this—have we not allowed such responsibility to slip away? Must we not somehow justify not only responsibility for an aspect of belief formation or retention, but also responsibility for belief *itself*?

Let me address these concerns by turning at once to our main case in point. Assuming Hitler to be at least a somewhat sane individual, it is not very likely to be true that he could have *virtuously* held to these beliefs. For instance, could Hitler have conscientiously believed in the authenticity of the Protocols of Zion and the so-called International Jewish Conspiracy? This does not seem very likely. To that extent, then, I am in a position to claim here that the worrisome supposition does not remain, on reflection, all that worrisome. Either Hitler is only insane—a definite possibility but not one I am exploring in this study—or, as I have been assuming, he is not. If he is not insane, then it remains highly plausible to suppose that he is morally accountable for his actions by way of being epistemically (and morally) culpable for his beliefs.

4. The Kantian Analogy

In this section I will attempt to reinforce the important discussion of "care" in section 3.3 with a further analogy, this one drawn from Kant's moral philosophy. Here I want to use certain features of Kant's moral philosophy as a "model" for developing a parallel conception of belief. My aim in this endeavor, I readily acknowledge, will be to apply and extend, not to defend, Kant. But, as will be seen, the doctrines selected from Kant are sufficiently a part of almost *any* view of moral responsibility and freedom of action that I may surely make this claim: That if doxastic responsibility can be shown to be on as strong a footing as Kantian moral responsibility, we will have achieved some considerable advance for doxastic responsibility and its relation to doxastic freedom.

The first Kantian doctrine concerns the ultimate responsibility we bear for our *attitude* toward the moral law.[5] This attitude, which we are to bear toward the moral law, Kant terms "respect." Kant distinguishes "respect" most importantly in terms of what we are entitled to expect of a person: In the case of other motivational attitudes (those that are "mere inclinations"), we can say only that this individual did or did not happen to have the attitude in question toward some given object. Respect is different; respect alone is something we can expect, something we can *require* of every rational being. It is a motivation, or a kind of motivation, that presupposes nothing about the character of an agent's inclinations, but instead simply that an agent understand and recognize the bearing of the moral law on her conduct. Thus, the excuse that "I just didn't feel like doing my duty," if it is meant to invoke a sense that one lacked adequate motivation for doing what was right, according to Kant, we perceive as not only implausible, but also as radically out of place.

The second point to be made is more a clear implication, than an explicit doctrinal part of a Kantian system of ethics; yet it is of crucial importance. Obviously, moral responsibility cannot consist entirely in one's attitude toward the moral law (or such surrogate abstractions as "morality" or "the good"). Somehow, that is to say, our attitudinal responsibility must be translated into responsibilities for what we *do* or fail to do. How, though, is this to be accomplished? In a Kantian system, this would be done most persuasively as follows. We *express* our respect for the moral law most importantly through the particular acts we will or refrain from willing. Notice, the point is *not* that we bear a primary responsibility for our attitude toward the moral law and a merely derivative responsibility for what we will. It is, instead, that I show what my real attitude towards the moral law is *through* my volitions, through the state of my will. Thus, my attitudinal responsibility and my volitional responsibility are the same. I bear a direct responsibility for both. Put otherwise, the attitudinal notion of a "due respect for the moral law" coincides with the volitional notion of "willing the right act." If I fail to will what is right, I thereby stand accused of failing to exhibit a due respect for the moral law on that occasion.

Now let us apply each point in the case of belief.

First, it is clear that the *content* of our norms governing belief is not the same as the content of our norms governing action. But this difference of content—of subject matter—hardly implies that the *nature* of our responsibilities must differ in the two cases. The mere fact that one content involves a basic regard for truth and the other—let us suppose, following Kant—a basic regard for other persons should not imply that the responsibility we bear in the one case is any greater or any more direct than the responsibility we bear in the other. On the contrary, because both contents involve eminently worthy, although different, objects, each of which we

are eminently capable of respecting, one would think that they
would be on a par, at least so far as our responsibility for respecting them is concerned.

Here, though, an objection may be raised.

> Surely, it is wrong to argue that because we can be held
> responsible for an attitude of respect for one thing, we can
> be held responsible for the same attitude toward something
> else. Many will hold, for persuasive reasons, that an attitude
> of respect is owed our Creator. Surely, it does not follow that
> we are responsible for whether we bear the same attitude
> toward, say, an earthworm.

This objection, however, overstates the nature of the inference I
want to make. I take it as evident that we *do* owe respect both to
moral and epistemic norms. I am only inferring that if we can be
responsible in a certain way in the one case, we can be responsible
in that same way in the other; that the mere shift of *content* should
imply no shift in the nature or extent of our responsibilities for
having this attitude.

Let us move on to the second point of our analogy. We have
observed that responsibility for one's attitude toward the moral law
is of obscure and uncertain application except in terms of one's
actual choice of an action (i.e., except in the context of one's will).
And there is, it seems, an analogous point to be made in the case
of belief: we "express"—to use the term used earlier in connection
with Kantian respect—our general regard for the truth *through* the
particular items we accept or reject (on the basis of whatever evidence we have or do not have for these items). In other words, a
generalized respect for the truth, like a generalized respect for
morality or the moral law, significantly enters into our normative
assessments of ourselves and others only insofar as it manifests
itself in the propositions one accepts as true or the actions one aims
to perform (although, again, each in the light of the evidence or
reasons one has for adhering to them). In *both* cases, then, what
we see is that direct responsibility for the having of a normatively
correct attitude, far from being incompatible with a direct responsibility for the proper expression of this attitude, requires such
responsibility.

5. Responsibility and "Avoidability"

In the history of modern philosophy, issues of the responsibility
for *x* are hardly separable from issues concerning the avoidability

of *x*. If I am to be held responsible for *x*-ing—and especially if I am to be held *culpable* for *x*-ing—the pervasive idea is that I must have, or have had, the capacity to avoid *x*-ing. Otherwise, it would appear, the appealing maxim that "ought implies can" is violated. This general concern, not surprisingly, has direct relevance in the present connection. One can imagine the following objection being raised to our notion of direct doxastic responsibility.

Even if one were otherwise sympathetic to your notion of a direct responsibility for an epistemically virtuous attitude and for its expression in belief, there remains the crucial question of whether, at any given point, one could have been maintaining a different attitude from the one that one is maintaining. If my attitude at any given point is one of insufficient care or concern, how am I to *change* this without the self-directed action that, you claim, is not the primary object of responsibility here? Surely if I do nothing, at best I can (passively) *hope* that my attitude will change. And if that is all I can do, or be expected to do, on what grounds can I ultimately be blamed or faulted for the beliefs that may issue from that faulty attitude?

Now, in reply I will admit that there is something right in this objection. Clearly, if I am not in a state that I am supposed to be in, my responsibility *becomes* one of bringing it about that I get into that state. Admittedly, my responsibility is not, at that point, one of simply "wishing and hoping" that my mental state will change. But let us also be clear on the difference between one's *primary* responsibility in any given situation and one's secondary or "contrary-to-duty" obligations, should that primary one remain unfulfilled.

Suppose that a gardener's (primary) obligation was to turn on the hose at time *t*, but failing that, to go through a special procedure *S* that would allow him to turn on the system after *t*. Here if the gardener fails to carry out his primary responsibility, he must try to bring about the same result but now by an indirect means. Now consider the analogous point.

The gardener cannot be held directly responsible for turning on the hose at *t*, for if he fails to do so, he can accomplish this result only by the indirect means *S*. At most the gardener can be held responsible for the relatively indirect, not the relatively direct, way of turning on the water.

Well, this obviously just begs the question, for it assumes that if the gardener does not turn on the hose at *t*, he could not. Likewise, it seems to me that the above objection supposes, in effect, that if my degree of virtue at any given point is not as it should be, it could not have been so. But what is the argument for that? It is certainly not part of our notion of care, that we cannot ever have been, not even under favorable circumstances, any more careful than in fact we have been.

We have perhaps won a battle, or a skirmish, but there remains the much larger question of whether epistemically virtuous—or, more to the point, nonvirtuous—attitudes *are* avoidable. This is a large question and I may perhaps be excused at this point in the discussion a brief excursus into questions of responsibility and avoidability as they come down to us in regard to action and choice—rather than belief. After all, it is in connection with these topics, and not belief, that these questions have traditionally been explored.

Let us begin, then, with a radical "libertarian" view and its most obvious—and arguably least tractable—difficulty. The radical libertarian holds that we are responsible only for those events that lack a cause—besides the agent himself or herself. But if our acts (or, alternatively, our choices, decisions, volitions) are thus left causally unconnected to the states that might have motivated and served to explain, in a comprehensible fashion, why we did them, the nature of our *responsibility* for these events must be left similarly unclear. The radical libertarian, for instance, will allow—in fact, insist—that if I am responsible for having chosen rightly when my motives were good, that I might have made the very same choice (and deserved the same credit for it) even if the general character of my desires had been bad. Such a choice, however, in the absence of appropriately decent desires (motives) seems more a miracle than something for which I would seem to deserve credit. (See Hobart [1934] for a classic statement of this viewpoint.)

In the case of belief, the issue appears to arise in an analogous way. Here the counterpart of an act (or the choice of an act) would seem to be the formation or rejection of a given belief content. The analogue of the factors bearing on choice (motives, intentions, etc.) would then be one's reflections on whatever considerations might possibly affect whether one believes a given item. Now, as in the case of action, it is intelligible that a given set of considerations might result either in one's accepting or rejecting *p* as true. The *difficulty* again concerns the problem of assigning positive and negative responsibility (praise and blame). First, again suppose that I were in every respect admirable for my belief in p, based on my evaluation of evidence q. Now suppose that this same (admirable) process resulted in the absence of this belief—at the last instant I just rejected p. Perhaps this scenario is intelligible, although I would question even this. (Could I in just the same total frame of mind accept or reject p?) But the key point is that, typically, if I were going to be criticized for rejecting p, this criticism would point to something defective either in my evaluation of the evidence—perhaps some logical error, perhaps something wrong with the frame of mind in which I conducted this evaluation process. Typically, the criticism would not be *simply* that I had failed to accept p. Likewise, if a thoroughly reprehensible process of evaluation had resulted in the formation of a belief for which I deserve condemnation, the contrary supposition—that I had at the last moment believed rightly—raises the same puzzle. If praise for my correct belief must be cut off from praise for the antecedent process of evaluation leading to it, this praise seems empty because it is groundless.

For this reason, one may wish to reject this kind of libertarian conception of belief formation and responsibility for same. Yet, of course, as the analogy with action would suggest, a nonlibertarian approach is likely to have a fundamental difficulty of its own. Such views characteristically hold that agents are only able to do otherwise (or choose otherwise) in the "iffy" sense that they would have done (or chosen) otherwise had antecedent conditions been different from the way that they actually were (see, for instance, Moore [1912, ch. 6]). Thus, relative to a given set of causal antecedents (considered as fixed), the nonlibertarian must concede that only one choice is causally possible; thus, that if this choice were something we would want to blame the agent for, we must be able to blame a person for something that, at the time of action, was causally impossible for him to avoid.

Again, the application of this to the case of belief is plain enough, at least in its main outlines. How can I be blamed for believing what, given my total psychological state, it was causally necessitated that I believe? Where I am criticized for believing p rather than q, how are we to maintain that I ought to have believed q when it does not seem that at the time I formed the belief that p, it was still causally possible for me to believe that q? In the case of action, "compatibilists" have argued, as just indicated, that one's "ability to do otherwise" in any such case is always to be understood conditionally—as meaning that "if conditions had been different (in some suitable way), one's action would have been different. Let us see how such a view might work out in the case of belief.

Suppose that a person, who is guilty of a lapse of attention, forms an incorrect belief that *p*. The person may condemn himself, saying (correctly, I shall assume)

(i) If I hadn't had a lapse of concentration, I would have realized that not-*p*.

But if (i) is intended in self-condemnation, presumably he will also assert

(ii) I could have concentrated more fully.

We now ask whether (ii), in turn, can be plausibly represented as a conditional, say, as

(iii) If I had tried to, I would have concentrated more fully.

Again, though, if (iii) is meant in self-condemnation, presumably this individual will allow that

(iv) I could have tried to concentrate harder.

But can this, in turn, be rendered by a further conditional? For instance,

(v) If I had wanted to, I would have tried to concentrate harder.

Again, if this is true, presumably I condemn myself because

(vi) I could have wanted to try to concentrate harder.

But clearly now we are nearing the end of analysis—if we have not already reached it. First, it is not clear that a person would condemn herself for not wanting to try as opposed simply to *not trying*. Take a comparable case of action. If I condemn myself for not trying harder to win a certain race, it would be obscure to insist that what I am really condemning myself for not wanting to try. I say this basically for two reasons: First, in a sense I certainly *wanted* to try my hardest, but I simply didn't have it within me to translate this desire into genuine effort. Second, if it is insisted, though, that if I had *actively* wanted to try, there would be no problem about translating this desire into genuine effort, there is an even more telling point to be made: namely, that there is no evident difference between actively wanting to try and just plain *trying*; hence, there is no point to distinguishing responsibility at the level of (iii) and (iv) from that of (v) and (vi). In other words, we might as well accept responsibility for not trying harder as *fundamental*.

Now, the question arises as to whether, absolutely, it is within one's power (at a given point) to have tried harder, to have exerted a greater concern for, in this case, the truth. Does one ever have a causal power either to be or not to be so concerned? Does one ever have it fully within one's power to instantiate either one of these states? Here I would only want to make two further points. The first is that we cannot now, and presumably never will, know with assurance whether this is possible. The second is that we are in exactly the same position in this regard as we are in regard to one's moral attitudes. As the Kantian analogy of section 3.4 attempted to bring out, an epistemically concerned attitude regarding the truth is like an ultimate attitude of respect for morality (the moral law). Whether the individual who fails to display, at a given time, a due respect for moral concerns absolutely could have done so is equally, as Kant himself confesses, something we do not know. We *assume* so of course, and we find this assumption natural, perhaps even irresistible (at least in our unguarded, philosophically unsophisticated moments). But that, of course, hardly passes for proof. The two questions of our powers with respect to these attitudes are, it seems to me, closely connected. The notion of such an absolute power—to have brought about something *else* without there having been any different conditions then obtaining—is a difficult one for common sense to fathom. But so is the notion that one's current level of effort, moral or epistemic, is so fixed by the conditions now obtaining that, truly, one can never try any harder than one is currently trying.

What we have found, then, is simply that the *analysis* of doxastic responsibility ends in precisely the place where our underlying view would have supposed it to end: namely, with the question of one's responsibility for exerting some reasonable effort in regard to the truth. But whether this effort should be understood as uncaused (by prior events and states) or as caused, say, by a combination of one's background epistemic character and certain locally variable conditions, I am not prepared to say. I will, as indicated, continue to excuse myself by saying that I have wished only to put doxastic responsibility on the same footing as actional responsibility, not to solve a problem for belief that has defied solution in the case of action for two thousand years.

Notes

1. Here and throughout this study, "direct responsibility for *x*" means simply responsibility that is not responsibility for doing something that causes *x*. This is the sense in which, I argued in chapter 1, we need to accord individuals direct responsibility for what they believe. This is the sense in which I will argue, in this and the next chapter, that we have direct responsibility for belief. Such a notion of "direct responsibility," or, relatedly, of something's being directly within one's power, is basically that of current action theory (see particularly Davidson [1971] on the difference between "*x*-ing" and "doing something which causes *x*").

2. I am assuming here, it should be noted, that Mary's belief that she would recover would not itself aid in her recovery (and that Mary has no reason to think that it would). But suppose this were otherwise on both counts. What about those interesting "bootstrap cases" in which one's having adequate evidence that *p* is contingent, wholly or partly, on one's already acquiring the belief that *p*? (Of course, the most famous of these is given in James's [1897] "Will to Believe.") Can and should an epistemically responsible person believe *p* on the strength of such belief-contingent reasons? This type of case is more like that of the ailing scientist than might first appear. For if I will only *appreciate* the force of certain possible evidence for *p* upon believing that *p*, I cannot be led in the usual way to accept *p* by the apparent strength of this evidence. Instead, I must indirectly cause myself to believe *p*, knowing (or believing) that if I do believe *p*, the evidence for *p* will emerge. The same, I will argue, is true of Mary's case even without this complication. But the Jamesian case of evidence that will come in only after one's belief does bring out one interesting point. Assuming that it would be irrational for a person not to get himself to believe that *p* under these conditions, we see that sometimes it is irrational *not* to believe in the face of the evidence (as one appreciates it). This, again, is not a counterexample to my original thesis because it involves, as Mary's case will, *acting* so as to alter one's beliefs, rather than believing in an immediate sense.

3. Earl Conee (1987) raises a challenging case—given what I am saying here—in which *p* is evident for a person, but in which this person also is aware that the very act of accepting *p* (as true) would render *p* false (thus render him guilty of accepting a falsehood). In such a case,

Conee argues, one's overriding commitment as a rational agent is to avoid acceptance of what is false, even at the cost of rejecting what is evident. From my standpoint, the question raised by Conee's case may or may not be the same as that raised by the Firthian case of Mary Curry. Insofar as an individual knows that accepting *p* will lead him to accept what is not true (i.e., insofar as he is at a moment focusing on that consideration), he may have it directly within his power not to accept *p*. But by the same token, under these circumstances this consideration—that accepting *p* would render *p* false—*does* function as a truth-related consideration pertaining to the very proposition whose possible truth one is entertaining. In this regard, it is nothing like the Firthian situation Mary Curry faces in which she is to accept what she has no direct reason for thinking true in the interests of securing knowledge of other, entirely different propositions in the future. What the Conee case does, I think, require (relative to my concerns here) is that one distinguish—more finely than I otherwise would have thought necessary—"evidence for *p*" (as it would normally be understood) and "reasons for thinking that a belief that *p* is true" (or, if one prefers to use Conee's term "reasons for thinking that acceptance of *p* would be acceptance of something true"). An immediate concern to apply epistemic virtue directly in the formation or retention of belief— the Conee case shows—may go beyond the usual sorts of evidentiary concerns and may embrace a broader notion of "reasons for thinking true." This, however, does not affect my conclusions regarding Firth's or any other case in which epistemic considerations of a longer-termed nature are involved.

4. Bernard Williams (1973) argues that any such strategy by which one seeks to convince oneself of something presently regarded as false would inevitably involve self-deception; Thomas Cook (1987) argues to the contrary. This issue, however, is peripheral to my concern here with the extent to which epistemic virtue may involve a kind of consequentialism (at the level of action, if not directly at the level of belief).

5. Cf. Kant's analysis in the *Critique of Practical Reason*, Bk. I., ch. 3. He writes: "In the subject there is no sensuous feeling tending to morality; that is impossible because . . . the incentives of the moral disposition must be free from every sensuous condition. Rather, sensuous feeling which is the basis of all our inclinations, is the condition of the particular feeling we call respect, but the cause that determines this feeling lies in the pure practical reason; because of its origin, therefore, this particular feeling cannot be said to be pathologically effected; rather it is practically effected" (p. 78).

Chapter Four

Epistemic Virtue and Responsibility II

Before proceeding, a brief review of the foregoing discussion and one important terminological clarification will prove helpful.

The first chapter argued that, mainly for purposes of moral responsibility, we need to hold individuals on many occasions responsible for what they believe and not only for the effect of their actions on what they believe. That is, we need to hold them directly rather than indirectly responsible for what they believe.

The second chapter introduced the notion of an epistemic virtue, distinguishing the overarching virtue of conscientiousness (a concern to find truth and avoid falsehood) from the various collateral virtues that seem necessary to ensure that conscientiousness itself is well employed. It was also observed, although we have not had and will not have occasion to make much of this notion,[1] that truth and the avoidance of error are not rich enough goals for the genuinely epistemically virtuous individual.

The third chapter tried to show—what is critically important to my overall argument—that in exercising these epistemic virtues in a doxastic context we are exerting a form of direct control over belief, albeit, as was also emphasized, an incomplete control.

The terminological point or clarification concerns the following difficulty. We have, as yet, no agreed-on term for what is the attitudinal modality or aspect of belief for which we are to be held directly responsible. It will not do to say, simply and without qualification, that we are responsible for being epistemically virtuous—not if that means *succeeding* in being an epistemically virtuous person—or even in functioning in a particular instance in the way that an epistemically virtuous person would function. For if we are talking about *responsibility*, as opposed to virtue itself, the most we can surely expect of a person is that he or she make some reasonable *effort* toward that end. In a full and unqualified sense of the term, being "epistemically virtuous," in other words, like being "morally virtuous," is not subject to our immediate control; one can only *try* (i.e., apply some reasonable level of effort). Whether this effort will succeed in truly constituting epistemic virtue is another question; certainly it is possible for an individual's conscious effort to arrive at truth and avoid prejudice to be undone by unconscious motivations and biases of a nonvirtuous sort. And, again, where this happens, it seems accurate to describe the situation as one in which an individual is trying but not entirely succeeding in being virtuous. Responsibility, in any case, must be keyed to the attempt rather than to the end result (given that the latter is not fully subject to our immediate control at any given point).

But this does not solve our terminological problem. What are we to call this "reasonable level of effort in regard to arriving at the truth?" We have variously described this in terms of an individual's displaying "care," "concern," or just "epistemic virtue" in her doxastic practices. But we have used no single term for this. Perhaps the best such term would be "conscientiousness," but we have already applied this to describe a particular epistemic virtue.

What I shall say, then, is this. I shall speak of our responsibility (for want of any better single term) as that of being epistemically virtuous or just virtuous. However, insofar as questions of responsibility are concerned, this use needs to be understood in terms of the immediately preceding discussion. This terminology is not meant to imply that we are expected to succeed in being epistemically virtuous but only in making some reasonable effort in this regard.[2] This choice has at least one advantage, which is that of reminding us that our efforts in regard to epistemic virtue are not limited to any particular virtue or attitude but may embrace any, although assuredly not at any given moment all, of the epistemic virtues. For instance, if we speak of a responsibility for being conscientious, this suggests—in line with the use of chapter 2—a focus on truth and the avoidance of error. But in any given instance there is no reason why an individual's focus should not be on, say, avoiding personal bias, or intellectual cowardice, or any other form of epistemic vice. These, however, are themes to be developed later (see especially section 4.3).

1. The Range of Doxastic Responsibility

I turn, then, to the main topic of discussion in this chapter: specifying at least the approximate range or extent of doxastic responsibility. If we are to make it entirely plausible that individuals are *responsible* for being virtuous in forming or examining their beliefs, we shall have to get substantially clearer about the conditions under which this responsibility holds. What attitudes are we typically responsible for maintaining in regard to our beliefs? How widely does this responsibility extend? Are we *always* responsible for being virtuous in our belief-forming activities. If not, under what typical conditions are we? And so forth.

In this regard, let me begin with an example of which I will want to make considerable use. It goes as follows. You are listening to the evening news. A man, who had been out on parole, is shown being arraigned for a series of brutal crimes. "They finally got him," you mutter, expressing your spontaneous belief that this is the man who had committed the crimes. Your reaction, again, was purely spontaneous, and, to that extent, we must allow, couldn't have been helped. Now, of course, someone *else*, hearing the same news might react reflectively. But that doesn't show that you could have done so; of course it shows only—what must qualify as a commonsense truth—that different people are likely to have different capacities for reflectiveness. Enter, though, your twelve-year-old child, who innocently asks you if this is the guilty man. You answer aloud and sincerely that we don't know whether he's guilty, that this will be settled at the trial. The question has *prompted* a virtuous response on your part. You are now not only capable of a virtuous response, you have actually given one. Now one last supposition. Suppose that when the child's question was raised, you had been in an unpleasant mood: you heard the question well enough, but did not particularly bestir yourself to think about it or its implications; you simply muttered, "Yeah, they finally got him." In this last case, I would want to claim, it is plausible to hold that you are *culpable* for not reconsidering your belief; for arguably (cf. the discussion of avoidability at section 3.5 and that of "negligence" at section 4.2) you could have done so, but you simply did not.

I see this small case as paradigmatic. Typically, it seems, we are able to be epistemically, or, for that matter, morally virtuous only when we have some special *reason* to be. To be sure, the effectiveness of such reasons varies with the individual, her emotional state, and much else. As we just saw, some persons might need a special reason to prompt their being virtuous, whereas others in the same situation might not. Still, the fact remains we that are basically creatures who exhibit, and are capable only of exhibiting, intellectual virtue when prompted to do so by some special reason. We are not creatures who maintain anything like a constant, even a constant minimal, level of such effort. (True, part of being conscious is maintaining a certain level of environmental *awareness*, but that is not the same thing as maintaining even a minimal level of epistemic virtue.)

Of course, it must be recognized that circumstances can also *impede* or even prevent outright a virtuous response that would otherwise have been forthcoming (even unprompted by other features of the situation). Circumstances may distract us (preventing adequate care); they may appeal to latent biases and enthusiasms (preventing us from exhibiting and even trying to exhibit due impartiality or sobriety); or, as in the preceding case, the immediacy of an environmental influence may preclude any degree of initial virtuous care. (This, of course, does not rule out later virtuous reflection as to whether this belief, suddenly acquired, should be *retained*.)

Again, though, I would insist that a plausible model of intellectual virtue will not see us as naturally given to this and deterred on occasion by an unfavorable environment but instead more the reverse: It will see us as naturally *not* given to this but instead as being prompted to more virtuous reflection (if at all) under those circumstances in which we are presented, or ourselves conceive, some special reason to be conscientious. Such reasons may be various. Under unusual circumstances, they might be general skeptical or Cartesian promptings toward more minimal claims about our world, but typically the relevant circumstances would be different. More typically, these would relate to the *practical* (e.g., the moral) consequences of our being wrong in a given instance. To revert to our previous stalking horse, when we hold Hitler responsible for a lack of epistemic virtue, our case is plausible insofar as Hitler presumably recognized the grave practical consequences of his beliefs, but was not evidently spurred by such awareness to anything like a satisfactory level of conscientiousness. These consequences, however, may be themselves epistemic; they may involve a recognition of the serious epistemic consequences of error (the scientist who must decide whether to accept or reject the results of an experiment that appears to defeat a cherished hypothesis).

One final observation in this connection. In many instances the mere thought of serious consequences might not be enough. A staunch believer in slavery presumably would only be jogged into further reflection by something fairly unusual, like the scene, which sometimes did excite spontaneous opposition to slavery even in the South, of a woman of very light complexion being sold down river to a buyer from New Orleans, well known for owning houses of prostitution.

As in the case of the moral virtues, it may be said, then, that we take the measure of persons according to how well they *respond* to such situations. Neither moral nor epistemic virtue consists in or requires the maintenance of anything like a constant, conscious attitude. Nor does the appropriateness of any particular response depend on one's having such an antecedent mental state. Here, though, the distinction—alluded to earlier—between virtue and responsibility becomes relevant. For whereas it is correct to estimate one's degree of virtue, at least in part, on the *basis* of one's capacity to respond, questions of responsibility are different. Here an individual must be judged *relative* to such capacities. If I am not capable of great generosity, that is obviously relevant to one's estimate of me, at the level of virtue, as an ungenerous person. But from the standpoint of responsibility, I can only be held culpable for my failures to exhibit the level of generosity of which I am now capable. And the same would be true in the case of the epistemic virtues.

Recognizing a distinction, then, between judging persons on the basis of, versus relative to, their underlying capacities to exhibit virtue limits the scope of our responsibility for being epistemically virtuous. Still, though, an objector may not be satisfied:

> It seems that there is a dilemma, or a kind of paradox, surrounding the notion of blaming a person for being epistemically unvirtuous. It runs as follows. If someone notices that he is not being, say, conscientious, or that he needs to be more so, this in itself impedes belief, preventing full conviction. But if a person does *not* notice this, he cannot be blamed for failing to be conscientious. For it would not seem that, having failed to notice this, he is capable of anything like a conscientious response.

The difficulty raised here appears serious, but the second horn of this dilemma is not perhaps as deadly as it might seem. For the question of culpability is *not* settled merely because an individual does not notice that conscientiousness (or any other given virtue) is called for. The question remains whether this individual *should* have noticed this. Quite possibly, her failure to notice this itself reflects some culpable lack of due care. Clearly, part of what is *wrong* with a Hitler is that, being unconscientious, he is not apt to notice when he is not being conscientious.

Yet the objector may continue, "So are you suggesting that we must go through life constantly on the alert for whether we are being adequately conscientious? I thought your model was, more plausibly, that *circumstances* are supposed to remind us of our unconscientiousness." Again, though, the objection is perhaps less serious than might appear. No, a constant state of alertness—in the sense of anything like a constant, active exertion of effort or care—is not required. What is required is a level of *responsiveness*, a readiness to respond to the ever-present possibility that special reasons for being conscientious will present themselves. Such readiness, however, is not the same as, and does not require being in, some particular constant mental state.

This last point is very important, so I shall try to underline it. Our model of doxastic responsibility should not explicitly or by implication expect too much or too little of ourselves. To expect a constant level of "active alertness" to the ever-present possibility that special efforts to be epistemically virtuous may be required, is too much. At the same time, we do not want to say merely because one did not perceive the situation to require special care that this excuses one's not giving such care. It seems to me that the safe and correct course between these undesirable extremes is to require, in effect, a certain responsiveness to the occurrence of conditions that may require a virtuous response but not to equate such responsiveness with anything like the active vigilance of a soldier on guard duty when an enemy attack is expected.

But all that having been said, an objector may still wish to venture further along this same line:

> Well, suppose an individual does not notice that circumstances call for a virtuous response simply because, *being* an epistemically unvirtuous person, he is not able to perceive this. Paradoxically, it will turn out that your theory, geared as it is to the concept of epistemic virtue, is unable to criticize precisely the individual who is epistemically unvirtuous.

My reply is just this. The objection begs the question of whether one's lack of epistemic virtue must be understood, at any given point, as an *incapacity* to be conscientious. For instance, imagine a corrupt politician who admits that he would have put forth a greater effort to resist the temptation of a bribe if only he had more clearly seen the desirability of such efforts. Being a corrupt politician, he pleads, he was unable to see this undesirability, and hence unable to resist temptation. The reply to such a person is that he could have and should have seen this desirability: "Being corrupt" need not be accepted as an excuse for the same reason that, say, "being lazy" need not. (We have little patience with the individual who says that "being lazy, I can hardly do more than lift a finger to help you. To do more would be out of character.") The claim that one is epistemically unvirtuous does not automatically deserve greater sufferance than these others.

Let me turn at this point to a different, although closely related, question. Under what conditions do we especially want or expect persons to be virtuous in the formation of their beliefs? This is closely related to our previous concern with the circumstances under which we are capable of being virtuous for one reason: We want and expect persons to be conscientious, it turns out, basically under just those conditions in which we are capable of being so. Why so? Because, as we have emphasized, typically what renders individuals capable of being conscientious are the presence of special *reasons* (based on their situation), for being so; and it will be based on these reasons that we would typically want and expect individuals to be epistemically virtuous.

This connection applies equally well where the reasons in question are practical and where they are epistemic (theoretical). For obvious reasons, in the previous example it was true that you ought not to tell your twelve-year-old that the man shown on television was guilty. Likewise, scientists may be given to all sorts of harmless and uncontrollable spontaneous promptings, as much so, I would guess, as nonscientists. But when one's beliefs really matter, say, when an important reading must be taken or a judgment made as to whether to take the results of a particular experiment seriously, one becomes capable of a careful, epistemically virtuous response—and, by the same token, we have good reason to expect such a response.[3]

Of course, the fit here is not entirely exact. There will be occasions when it would be a good thing for one to be virtuous, yet when one can't. Here assuming that "ought implies can," a virtuous effort must be deemed merely a good thing but is not *required*. In other situations, though, a person may be able to be virtuous without there being anything like reasons, all things considered, for her to be so. One may just "feel like" being conscientious and thus be eminently capable of being conscientious under circumstances in which one needs, for practical reasons, *not* to be so. A case in point: You are a philosophy major on the Carleton College varsity football team, listening to the coach's last minute pep talk. Of course, it is always epistemically a good thing to be conscientious, but this is not the place for it.

At this point, however, it may prove instructive to consider the following objection:

> Virtuously formed belief, on this account, is basically a drive to pursue the truth for its own sake. But you admit that we are, for the most part, only capable, and, more revealingly, that for the most part we really only *should* exhibit such virtue when we have some special reason to do so. Yet these special reasons turn out, just as one would expect, to pertain to some larger goal beyond the truth. So how exactly is it that epistemic virtue involves anything like valuing the truth in its own right?

In reply, I will say, first, that even when there is no special reason to be virtuous, a concern for truth remains a valid concern, and nothing I have said implies otherwise. But, more to the point, one needs to draw this distinction. Someone cannot exhibit genuine epistemic virtue without being motivated at some level by a regard for the truth. It is impossible—psychologically or conceptually—for one to be virtuous without such a regard. And this remains true even if—as I have also maintained—people are characteristically prompted to exhibit such virtue only when there exist special reasons to do so. Consider an analogy. Even if it were true that people were only obliged to be honest to one another when either someone might be hurt by a lie or the proposition in question related to some special subject matter, honesty itself could still be characterized as requiring a certain motivation, a certain orientation toward truth or the communication of truth. In other words, the point would be that it is only under certain circumstances that one is required to exhibit this motivation towards the truth.

2. Epistemic Negligence

It will deepen our insight into these and related matters if we measure this against some of what has been written about the legal and moral concept of *negligence*. For what, in effect, the failure to respond to one's circumstances in an appropriately virtuous way amounts to, of course, is a form of negligence. One might call it "epistemic negligence." But insofar as *all* negligence may be construed as a want of something like "due care," such epistemic negligence would not constitute a separate type of negligence, wholly disjointed from standard instances of negligence in the law.

Now, if we consult a stand legal treatment of negligence, William Prosser's (1971), we learn first that the legal standard of negligence is "external" or "behavioral" not "internal" or "psychological." Commenting on the adage that "Negligence is conduct, not a state of mind," Prosser writes:

> In most instances, it is caused by heedlessness or carelessness. But it may also exist where [the agent] has considered the possible consequences carefully, and has exercised his own best judgment. (p. 318)

Philosophically, one can agree that negligence is not to be equated with an *actual* state of mind. For example, a person might be insufficiently responsive to his situation and be in any one of a wide range of mental states. But I cannot agree that negligence is to be judged by a mere "objective standard of conduct" lest negligence fall unceremoniously into a form of "strict liability." If Jones has exercised her *best* judgment and still fallen short, then the law may hold her responsible for some omission on her part, but it should not hold her truly *negligent*.

In another interesting passage, Prosser writes:

> So far as perception is concerned . . . unless his attention is legitimately distracted, the actor must give to his surroundings the attention which a standard reasonable man would consider necessary under the circumstances, and that he must use such senses as he has to discover what is readily apparent. (p. 323)

This, I think, is good, but still a bit too "objective," at least from the highly theoretical standpoint of epistemology and moral philosophy. What I like is that one's degree of attentiveness is to be apportioned to the circumstances; it is very much a response to the needs of the situation and not the constant exertion of effort or even the constant exercising of a uniform habit. What bothers me is only the fact that underlying this sensitivity to circumstances is an underlying insensitivity to questions of whether a given person is capable of conforming herself to the standard of the "average person."

I find even more interesting in this connection a recent paper by Steven Sverdlik (1991) on blameworthy negligence, as he is sensitive to the same kind of dilemma we raised earlier concerning one's responsibility for responding to certain situations in an appropriately virtuous way. On Sverdlik's formulation, this dilemma comes out as follows. He contrasts two views of negligence: one in which negligence involves the deliberate *choice* at some earlier point to undertake a risk (e.g., deciding to have that third drink before driving home) and one in which negligence is simply undertaking what is objectively risky conduct but which one may have no *reason* for regarding risky. For Sverdlik, as one would expect, neither view is acceptable. The former describes, he says, "reckless but not negligent behavior"; the latter, conduct that scarcely seems culpable. Sverdlik's positive view, then, becomes this. Negligence involves having some "reason to believe" that a certain course of conduct is risky—such reason being grounded in one's own stock of *beliefs* concerning the matter in question. The negligent person, on this view, has beliefs sufficient to infer the dangerous or risky character of the behavior in question but fails to draw the appropriate conclusion from these beliefs. Insofar as he has such beliefs, he has reason to believe that this behavior is questionable, but insofar as he fails actually to draw this conclusion, he is merely negligent and not guilty of anything like deliberately reckless conduct.

Whereas I find Sverdlik's way of setting up the problem of negligence illuminating, I reject his solution on two counts. First—and admittedly this will require only a slight revision of his account—if one has the appropriate beliefs but is legitimately *unable* to draw the indicated conclusion, this should be exculpatory rather than grounds for a judgment of negligence. Second—and now penetrating to the heart of the matter—if one lacks the appropriate beliefs because of some avoidable lack of due care, clearly this should not excuse one. Again, Hitler cannot automatically excuse himself on grounds that, lacking the beliefs from which to draw morally acceptable conclusions, he was unable to draw these. My point, then, is that we must recognize underlying *attitude*, rather than one's current stock of beliefs, as the real issue.

I turn next to some comments on this subject of epistemic negligence made in the course of a much broader discussion by Robert Adams (1984, p. 11). Adams, like Sverdlik and myself, rejects the thesis that all epistemic negligence is ultimately caused by a want of due care in one's actions. Adams, however, moves immediately from this recognition to the view—very different from any taken here—that where such negligence is not due to any actional failure, it constitutes a "sin" for which one bears a kind of responsibility—but not a responsibility which requires that one could have *avoided* this state. A Hitler Youth, he says (drawing on an example of Alan Donagan [1977]), may have corrupt, sinful beliefs owing to the circumstances of his education—beliefs that he could not have avoided having.

What I want to say about such cases, however, is something different. I want to *preserve* the connection between fault and avoidability but maintain that not all avoidable faults are grounded in failures of action. Thus, even if the Hitler Youth is guilty of a kind of sin for which he is not (in a narrow sense) blameworthy—insofar as this is nothing he could have avoided—this is not for me the truly interesting issue. The interesting issue is whether he is not blameworthy for what may genuinely be avoidable, namely, his *continuing* to hold these beliefs and his acting on them. Insofar as this is true, the Hitler *Jugend* may not only be a sinner in Adams's basically theological sense but be, in nontheological terms, morally culpable as well.[4]

3. Further Problems

The account presented thus far has stressed the role of special reasons—prompting conscientious reflection—that serve to interrupt our otherwise untutored, largely unvirtuous responses to our environment. One question raised by this point of view, however, concerns *perception*. If perception is to play anything like the role accorded it by philosophers, psychologists, and common sense in the acquisition of knowledge, one wants to know whether considerations of epistemic virtue are applicable to perception.

I would answer along these lines. Immediate or spontaneous perceptual beliefs are not, as such susceptible of being virtuous or unvirtuous. In this respect, they are like one's untutored response to the criminal shown on the television news. Lacking anything to deter an immediate response, it will be the case that considerations of virtue and vice are not applicable at that immediate level. Here, however, a distinction needs to be drawn between the acquisition and *use* of such perceptual data. Obviously, most use of such data is not by way of immediate reflex; most such use does provide opportunity for reasons to prompt one to exhibit due care. One might spontaneously perceive a movement in the brush as a deer, but before shooting, one had better make sure that it is not a fellow hunter. Likewise, there can be special reasons to be careful even at the level of spontaneous perception. Recall the extreme case discussed in chapter 1 where a soldier was wired up in such a way that a gun would fire if he simply formed a relevant belief. In this case, one has a special reason to be as careful as possible that functions antecedently to any perception.[5] In general, though, it is at the level of use, rather than acquisition, that considerations of virtue and responsibility arise. (This, however, does *not* mean—as I was at considerable pains to argue in chapter 1—that responsibility arises at the level of action rather than belief. It means only that one's use of perceptually acquired information may be judged according to the degree of virtues this use involves.)

Another possible area of difficulty concerns the following problem, which we have already touched on in connection with the analysis of negligence in section 4.2. But the issue is sufficiently important to explore a different aspect of it here.

Recall our discussions of Iago and Hitler in sections 1.6 and 3.1; in these discussions, we tried to show that one could be responsible in a direct way for acting on, or exercising, a character trait for whose existence one was not directly responsible. But now the following objection arises. Iago, it may be objected, was a deliberate malefactor; Hitler, though, was not *deliberately* closed-minded or anything of the sort. His beliefs were, instead, influenced by deep prejudices, of which he was scarcely aware. Hence, although we can condemn his epistemic character as defective, there are no grounds here—the objection would have it—to blame Hitler for what he has done.[6]

The difficulty just raised is a general one, statable as the following argument:

(i) If we are ever culpable in regard to our beliefs, we are so in virtue of their determination by nonverific (non-truth oriented) rather than verific, motivation.

(ii) A person is only responsible for acting/believing on the basis of a motive *M* if, at the time he acts/believes he is aware of acting/believing on the basis of *M*.

(iii) When we believe on the basis of nonverific motives, of necessity we are not aware of this motivation at the time in question.

(iv) Therefore, we are never culpable in regard to our beliefs.

Such a conclusion would obviously be devastating for my entire project. But where do I think that this argument goes wrong? I certainly do not want to take issue with its first premise. After all, if a normative approach is to have any bite to it at all, it must criticize practitioners of wishful thinking and other forms of unconscientious belief. If a normative epistemological can't criticize the wishful thinker, who can it criticize?

What, then, of the third premise? There may be cases of something rather *like* deliberate unconscientious belief. This is a possibility we will want to consider further in the next chapter (section 5.2). Still, it can hardly be said that very much of what qualifies as, say, wishful or closed-minded thinking is deliberately so. In general, epistemic vice is *not* accompanied by any clear awareness of one's less-than-respectable motives. Somehow the wishful thinker is able to convince himself that what he is believing is genuinely true. Perhaps this is often a matter of self-deception; but certainly it is not always or necessarily so, and self-deception is hardly a classic instance of deliberate wrongdoing.

Of course, this leaves us with the second premise—and let me now try to explain where this one goes wrong. My starting point is that our doxastic responsibility is fundamentally a matter of having the right (epistemically virtuous) attitude. Now if I am motivated by other than virtuous concerns under conditions when I ought not to be so motivated, to the extent that I have led to this condition by my *failure* to maintain a properly virtuous attitude, clearly I am culpable. In short, even though I may be unaware of the operation of these nonverific motives, and certainly cannot be accused of having deliberately believed on the basis of them, I can be held culpable for their operation through my negligent failure to exhibit the right sorts of attitudes. Thus, the operation even of entirely unconscious prejudices can be subject to blame.

A third area requiring closer attention concerns the relation between conscientiousness and the other epistemic virtues—not now at the level of standing but at the level of qualities *exercised* in the formation, retention, and use of beliefs. What virtues are we typically expected to exhibit in these connections? How do these virtues relate to the "special reasons" we have been invoking throughout this chapter? How do the various "regulative" virtues figure in this connection in relation to the overarching virtue of conscientiousness?

Let me begin with this last concern. Typically, no doubt, reasons for being virtuous are, most directly, reasons for being conscientious (for believing what is true and avoiding what is false). In many instances, however, such a concern is hardly separable from some more specific concern relating to a particular regulative virtue. In our original example, I may respond to the twelve-year-old having, as it were, girded myself not to be precipitous or otherwise prejudiced in my beliefs. If these are characteristic vices of mine, it may be important that their avoidance is at the focal point of my attention (with the more abstract virtue of conscientiousness merely a background consideration).

Still, it must be noted that conscientiousness preserves what is in essence a privileged position in this sense. Mere reasons to exemplify some regulative virtue, which are not also reasons to be conscientious, are not reasons to be *epistemically* virtuous (even if they are reasons to be virtuous in some other sense). If, for instance, I have a special monetary incentive not to be precipitous or not to be prejudiced in my outlook, it may be well and good for me to focus on avoiding these vices, but this focus can hardly be termed an overall expression of epistemic virtue. Thus, even where one might be expected to place some other virtue, and not conscientiousness, at the forefront of one's consciousness—again, typically because the absence of such a virtue was liable to be a problem for one in the situation in question—this does not mean that conscientiousness fails to be required.

4. A Dialogue with the Cardinal

Having developed the notions of virtue and responsibility at some length now, perhaps it will be instructive, and may serve to relieve the tedium of unremitting analytical discussions, if we imagine how my developing account might fare under the onslaught of a John Henry (Cardinal) Newman,[7] a thinker with a detailed conception of belief and the processes leading to belief—but a conception that is evidently less rationalistic and less moralistic than my own.

Newman: What worries me, first, about your notions of conscientiousness and epistemic virtue is their abstractness. You are focusing on what is at most an *aspect* of the process by which beliefs are formed.

Montmarquet: I am aware of that. Like moral virtue, epistemic virtue is but part of a larger complex of thoughts and attitudes. I have not claimed otherwise.

Newman: But you write as though I had never refuted Locke (not to mention Descartes and Clifford) on the "ethics of belief" [cf. chapter VI, section 1].

Montmarquet: Indeed, and I write as though William Jennings Bryan had never refuted Darwin. Am I wrong?

Newman: Well, consider this. As Locke himself admits, we constantly assent without qualification or reservation to what has at most been established as a matter of probability. Yet Locke claims we ought always to proportion our degree of assent to the extent of the evidence.

Montmarquet: I'm afraid your refutation is less than stunning. All you seem to have established is that Locke holds that sometimes our doxastic tendencies are a bit excessive. If they were never so, what would be the point of an ethics of belief? My own reaction, personally, is that in these cases, the evidence may well be sufficient for full assent, even though it is not sufficient for one's being absolutely certain. Hence, if assent is apportioned to the evidence, full assent is not really out of place inasmuch as the evidence *is* sufficient for belief, even if it is not sufficient for a belief in the total certainty of the item in question. You understand, of course, the difference between a belief that *p* and a belief that *p* is absolutely certain.

Newman: But, getting back to Locke, he has in effect admitted that assent can be unconditional, even where one's degree of acceptance, relative to the evidence, is less than full.

Montmarquet: But of course assent can be unconditional where it shouldn't be so. That, again, is the main point of Locke's, Descartes', and Clifford's animadversions against one who goes beyond the evidence. Locke is not saying that assent is never full-out (the contrary of your own view that it is *always* full-out); he is observing that sometimes it is full-out when it *shouldn't* be.

Newman: Your point is well taken—as far as it goes. Still, what I want to maintain—against Locke, Descartes, Clifford, and apparently you as well—is that we do not *characteristically* arrive at our beliefs in anything like the rationalistic way all of you seem to propose. Now, you may say that, all the same, humankind *should* believe in this way. But I reply that it doesn't, and that we are better off for it. Recall, for instance, my discussion of the simple and advantageous faith of the early Christians [chapter VII, section 1].

Montmarquet: Like many of your commentators, I'm puzzled at this point whether you're defending outright unthinking assent or assent for perhaps less than logically conclusive reasons.

Newman: Both, for each is valuable in its place. Simple unreflective certainty—what I call "virtual" or "interpretive" certitude—is a virtue in many believers. But it is not, I agree, a source of knowledge. As to knowledge, I also want to say that this generally results not from any application of virtuous effort not to go beyond the evidence, but, on the contrary, from a confident application of one's powers of judgment [cf. the discussion of Aristotle's *phronesis*, ch. IX, section 1].

Montmarquet: I have read your discussion of this "illative sense" and I admire you anticipation of much recent discussion (mostly by the philosophical foes of artificial intelligence) of the irreducibility, or alleged irreducibility, of cognition to the following of specifiable rules and recipes. But let me introduce two important variables into the picture. First, there is an important difference between, on one hand, one who clearly *sees*, where others do not, the way to a solution of a complex problem and, on the other, those who have (or think that they have) some special sense or "intuition" of the right solution, without clearly seeing how (or even that) it is right. Second, there is a difference, especially in the latter case, between one who relies on his *first* (as yet unproven powers of intuition) and one who relies on this power once it has been reasonably proven. Now, the general claim I would wish to suggest is this. Whether one has a *right* to be sure—whether or not one's belief is formed in a truly conscientious way—properly depends not on its following in some specifiable way from general rules but *does* depend very much on the two aforementioned variables. Reliance, for instance, on "blind intuition" may begin in a form of intellectual fanaticism but end in perfect intellectual responsibility once it becomes clear, through experience, that this intuition is reliable.

Newman: What, then, is your point—or criticism?

Montmarquet: Fundamentally, it is that you have not established that what you regard as desirable cases of intellectual conduct do not involve conscientiousness. To take one of your favorite examples, you fail to establish that Napoleon was unconscientious in relying on his own judgment, say, at Austerlitz.

Newman: Are you suggesting that Napoleon, in the heat of the battle, was making a special effort to proportion his belief to the evidence?

Montmarquet: He would have been unconscientious if he treated certain matters of probability as if they were certainties.

Newman: But doesn't the great gambling commander do precisely that? Think of Lee dividing his already too small army at

Chancellorsville, sure that Hooker's inability to act would give Stonewall Jackson time to launch a surprise attack from the rear.

Montmarquet: You are confusing a calculated risk and an illusion of certainty. The great commanders were aware of the limitations of their evidence, but appreciated at times the necessity of risk taking, especially when (as in Lee's case) they knew themselves to be at a strategic disadvantage. If their confidence was excessive at times, *that* was no practical virtue—or haven't you heard of Waterloo or Pickett's Charge? Realize the fact that cognitive solutions are often not derived in purely logical, deductive ways does not imply that these are somehow intellectually irresponsible or unconscientious. On the contrary, however a solution is derived, the morality and practicality of acting on it are very much dependent on a due assessment of its degree of certainty.

Newman: But admit that the great problem solvers, in all the various fields, have not been focused on restraining themselves to stay within the evidence. Such a negative orientation can hardly succeed in getting one anywhere.

Montmarquet: I admit that the problem solving phase itself is not mainly to be characterized by restraint or what I called the virtue of "sobriety." At this stage *other* epistemic virtues such as intellectual courage properly dominate. But now you are focusing on what is but an aspect of the larger whole. Obviously, there is more to epistemic virtue than mere restraint. Please do not confuse epistemic virtue with philosophical skepticism; they are not the same.

Notes

1. The relevant point here can perhaps best be put in terms of the distinction drawn earlier between reasons to believe a given item *true* and reason to *get* oneself to believe a given item true. (Compare in this regard the entire discussion of section 3.2, including the related notes.) Reasons based on long-term epistemic goals rather than truth, it may be seen, generate reasons only of the latter sort. The fact that *p* (*if true*) would greatly expand our knowledge is certainly not a reason to believe that *p is true*, although conceivably it could be a reason to act in ways that might get one to believe that *p* is true.

2. There is a question of what *level* of effort (to be virtuous) we are expected to give. Is merely some "reasonable level" sufficient, or must one, say, literally "try one's hardest?" My answer is basically that the difference between "one's best" and a "reasonable" level of effort is not clear in this regard. I will readily grant, with Bernstein (1986), that one

can distinguish between *actions* that are epistemically obligatory (say, checking some relevant quote once) and actions that would be supererogatory from an epistemic standpoint (checking that same quote a second time). But at the level of *belief* formation, such a difference becomes harder to discern. On this level, the most apparent difference is between the absence of any particular effort and the exertion of some reasonable effort, which is also likely to constitute the best that one could do under the circumstances.

3. See Stevenson (1975, pp. 254–56) for a more general discussion of the kinds of reasons that bear on scientists' not only acting, but also believing, conscientiously.

4. Also worthy of discussion in this connection are the views of Holly Smith (1983), briefly commented upon in chapter 1.

Smith's view of "culpable ignorance" is dominated by a conception of doxastic responsibility that Sverdlik and Adams reject, and which I took some pains to refute in section 1.3. For Smith, culpable ignorance involves a situation in which some culpable act is grounded in a lack of knowledge for which the agent is to blame. In particular, Smith requires that these three features be present: (i) one's culpable act must be justified relative to one's beliefs; (ii) one's culpable act must be done under circumstances when further investigation of these (ignorantly held) beliefs is no longer possible or desirable; and (iii) there must be some earlier "benighting act" (or omission) that is the cause of one's ignorance (pp. 145–47).

Clause (iii) explicitly invokes the kind of "actional" view of doxastic responsibility I have attempted to refute, but notice that clause (ii) seemingly has the same effect. For why require that it be, in effect, too late for further investigation unless one thinks that if there were time for such investigation, one's real fault would be one of failing to carry out this investigation? Compare on this point my own view (defended at section 1.3): Even where a person has the opportunity to conduct further tests on his beliefs, typically if he does not do so, this is because he *believes*—in some cases culpably—that further tests are not necessary.

As noted in chapter 1, Smith's final view of culpable ignorance is based on a conception of *blaming*, according to which actions are blameworthy only if motivated by some "reprehensible configuration of desires and aversions." But why cannot an action be blameworthy owing to some purely cognitive failure? Smith answers that those who believe that culpable ignorance does not excuse also believe that various *other* noncognitive, nondesiderative deficiencies (such as drunkenness) do not excuse, "they must offer us a unified theory to cover all the cases in which they want to blame the agent for his act" (p. 562). Because Smith finds no such theory forthcoming, she feels entitled to disregard the aforementioned claims only behalf of cognitive deficiencies.

My comments are the following. First, since those who hold that cognitive deficiencies render one blameworthy may very well *not* want to hold that these other noncognitive, nondesiderative states confer blame, Smith's reply is rather limited in the scope of its effectiveness (it is seriously *ad hominem*). What is worse, Smith's demand for a "unified theory" seems misconceived. The view against which she is arguing is one that assigns blame *any* later act whose harmful (or other morally negative) character is caused by some earlier, culpable act. (The range of causes, Smith notes, may be wide enough to cover anything from desiderative to cognitive to entirely nonmental causes—as when an earlier error leads defective *equipment* to cause a later action to misfire.) It is unclear, however, why this is not as much of a unified statement as would be *natural* to expect from such a view. Its claim, after all, *is* that what unites these cases is a causal attribute—and not anything like a "natural kind" or intrinsic similarity among these causes.

5. Strictly, though, I would not want to say that spontaneously formed belief can never be susceptible of conscientious efforts. Suppose, for instance, that quiz contestants are giving rapid answers to questions about U.S. presidents. Their answers may be immediate (time does not permit reflection), yet they may be subject to a greater or lesser degree of conscientious effort. See the discussion of this in my 1987b.

6. Compare in this regard Evans's (1963, pp. 145–46) attempt to refute Descartes on the grounds that error cannot be voluntary and O'Hear's highly pertinent reply (1972, section 1). Descartes himself addresses this issue at HR II, p. 224.

7. The dialogue below is drawn loosely from Newman's *An Essay in Aid of a Grammar of Assent*. More specific references are bracketed in the text. Useful discussions of Newman's theory may be found in Price (1969, lecture 6), Pojman (1986, chapter 10), and Jay Newman (1986, p. 127).

Chapter Five

Doxastic Voluntariness

It does *seem* and it has certainly seemed to many recent philosophers[1] that belief is not subject to our voluntary control. Thus, John Heil (1983a) writes that the "*phenomenology* of belief . . . as distinct from its epistemological conceptualization [i.e., the way epistemologists have typically conceived belief], looks distinctly non-voluntary" (p. 357). For Heil, our beliefs "seem mostly *forced* on us [or] if that is too strong, they come to us unanticipated and unbidden." This alleged involuntariness of belief, moreover, can and has been urged as the basis for a conclusion that would be singularly destructive of the main contentions of the present study. It will be said that since we are not able to exert anything like a direct voluntary control over what we believe, that we lack anything like a corresponding direct responsibility for those beliefs. So a great deal of what I have said, and will want to say, appears to hang on the present issue. How do I deal with the problem of voluntariness?

Basically in two ways. First, I will construct a notion of voluntariness that, I will allow, *is* required for doxastic responsibility. In this *weak* sense, I will show, many beliefs do qualify as voluntary. Second, I will distinguish a stronger notion of doxastic voluntariness that, I concede, may not be realizable, but which is also demonstrably not required for doxastic responsibility.

I will begin, though, with some more general reflections on what inclines many theorists to classify beliefs as involuntary. First, for all sorts of claims, such as that I am ten feet tall, it is simply not possible for me to get myself to believe them however hard I may try and however much reason (practical reason) I have to believe them. Moreover, and much more to the present point, it is certainly not possible in the case of such claims to simply adopt them "at will" (i.e., believe them on the simple condition that one wants to

79

believe them). I may indeed try to get myself to believe that I am ten feet tall, say, by going to a hypnotist who will seek to convince me of this, but I can hardly just accept this proposition at will. That much is clear.

To all of this, however, there is a possible reply. Whereas it is true that we are unable to bring ourselves to believe (at will) what we regard ourselves as having no reason, or no good reason, to think true, the same is true, *mutatis mutandis*, for the case of action. If we really have no reason to do something, say, run head-on into a nearby wall, it also seems that we are, in one perfectly valid sense, unable to do it. And if this is correct, one may wish to conclude that belief and action form two parallel systems, each subject to its own distinctive influence (actions to reasons for doing and belief to reasons for thinking true) with neither system necessarily exhibiting any more voluntariness than the other.[2]

This, however, is hardly the end of the matter. Take a case in which I seem to have equally good reason to do either of two incompatible acts, say, at this moment, standing up or remaining seated. Here I may simply choose to do either one. Is there any doxastic analogy to this, it may be wondered? Arguably, there is not. If I have equally good reason to accept either of two incompatible beliefs, presumably I should endorse neither. If, on the other hand, I have equally good reason to believe *p* and *not* to believe *p* (as opposed to believing not-*p*), then presumably I should believe something weaker, perhaps that *p* and not-*p* are equally probable. In short, it seems that we are compelled to *fit* our beliefs to the world in a way in which we are not compelled—in fact cannot—fit our actions to the world. With equally good reason to *say* "heads" or "tails" I can simply say one or the other. But with equally good reason to believe that one will come up as the other, I cannot simply choose what to believe. Rather, my beliefs are constrained to fit my assessment of the evidence in a way in which my actions are not constrained to fit my reasons for them.

Why this interesting difference? One conjecture I find plausible would be this. In the case of belief there is only one conscious, controlling value, which is truth. We may negligently fail to pursue this value, we may unconsciously pursue other ends in our belief-forming practices, but truth remains, in that special sense, the controlling value. In the case of action, however, there is no such value singularity. There are several independent value frameworks: morality, prudence, selfish short-term interests, and others. There is also within each broader category the real possibility of incommensurable value differences.[3]

Belief, I concede, then, is involuntary insofar as it seems to be controlled by a single value. (Whether one can consciously strive to believe for reasons other than truth I shall come back to in section 5.2.) Still, this does not mean—and now I am introducing the subject of "weak voluntariness" to be explored in the next section—that we are not able to distinguish levels of voluntariness with respect to this single value. Roughly, the idea will be this. There are circumstances that permit an unimpeded attempt to find truth and there are circumstances, closely analogous to those that impede voluntariness in the case of action, that do impede this attempt. "Weak voluntariness," then, is basically the relative absence of such factors. It is not the same thing as genuine voluntariness (in the full sense in which actions are voluntary), for, as I have already indicated, such weak voluntariness would not require the presence of any true doxastic *choice* (on a level with actional choice).

1. Weak (Analogical) Doxastic Voluntariness

Abstracting from the previously noted difference between systems admitting of but a single controlling value and systems of genuine choice, I want to be exploring in this section what factors are typically regarded as undermining or inhibiting the voluntariness of action, and exploring the extent to which these have doxastic analogues.

To begin, let us observe that a major factor limiting the voluntariness of action are the interferences, especially the coercive interferences, of other agents. Although difficult questions lurk here (cf. Nozick [1969]) concerning the definition of coercion and the extent to which noncoercive offers (e.g., of large bribes) may also limit voluntariness, it is fairly well agreed, at least, that outright coercion and other forms of control of one agent by another limit the voluntariness of actions. Does belief admit of similar forms of control? It would seem so. First there are cases of 1984-type mind control. In fact many cases of involuntary action (e.g., of the "Manchurian Candidate's" type) are so precisely because the action is founded on what may be termed an involuntary *belief*. The attempt, however, to influence belief in basically coercive ways is hardly limited to such extreme cases. Even if we do not count "rational argument" as coercive, our world is replete with other forms of doxastic control, using nonrational (or subrational) fears, hopes, and, in the most general of senses, associations to achieve its ends.

Second, actions may also be involuntary because of the effects of external factors in addition to human agents. Aristotle's case of throwing one's goods overboard in a storm (*N. Eth.*, Bk. III, ch. 1) would be as good an example as any here. He writes that such actions are involuntary inasmuch as "in the abstract no one throws away goods voluntarily" but voluntary inasmuch as they are "worthy of choice at the time they are done."

Beliefs, likewise, admit of such external constraints. Consider Terri, who is working on a term paper concerning the Mayan Indians. Owing to factors beyond her control, Terri has only one day left to do this entire project—research and writing. To make matters worse, she is unable to get to her campus library and has only the resources of the neighborhood children's library. In the course of doing this hurried project, Terri may well form some untoward beliefs about the Mayans, beliefs due mainly to her exigent circumstances. Terri is aware of these circumstances and the effect they are likely to have on her beliefs, but she is able to make allowances for this only to a certain extent. Beyond that, her beliefs are heavily the product of this intellectually limited and emotionally straining experience.

Third, we may notice that an involuntary action may result simply from some "mechanical failure" in the various systems and subsystems that underlie or that must carry out an intentional action. In a typical case, I reach out to take a cup of coffee then, surprised at how hot it is, involuntarily drop it. There can also be failures on more fundamental levels. A stroke victim might intend to say or do one thing and involuntarily say or do something different. A sufferer from Alzheimer's disease might have forgotten that the person next to him is his wife, then order this supposed stranger from his home, thus involuntarily ordering his own wife out of his house.

There are also doxastic analogues to this third sort of involuntariness. In the immediately preceding case, for instance, the Alzheimer's sufferer formed what could be fairly described as an involuntary belief, owing to a diseased and defective memory, that this woman lives somewhere else. Inasmuch as beliefs are the result of certain internal operations of the brain, there is hardly a limit to what internal malfunctions might produce the oddest notions—which we witness in the case of insane and mentally disabled people. At its most extreme, a person might go "completely mad," losing all control over his system of beliefs.

Fourth, and here we go back to Aristotle again, it is notable that ignorance often creates involuntariness in action. Being ignorant of some key facts, Oedipus involuntarily killed his father and involuntarily married his mother.

But can there be any doxastic analogues here? Mere ignorance of some fact would not seem to make a belief, formed on the basis of other facts, "involuntary," even in an extended sense. Oedipus's belief that Jocasta was unrelated to him was, if you will, "ignorant," but it was not for that, I think, involuntary. Still, where ignorance infects one's knowledge of the basis of one's belief, then it does seem to affect its voluntariness. Thus, take the case of James, a summer intern for the Tobacco Institute. In the course of his summer work, which is not directly related to issues concerned with whether cigarettes are a health risk, James is surprised to find many his previous antismoking beliefs have changed. He credits this to such factors as his respect for the senior scientists he works with, all of whom, he is aware, accept the tobacco industry's "line" on smoking and health. James has, it seems, involuntarily acquired certain beliefs, in part, through being (at the time of their operation) ignorant of the causes inducing him to form these beliefs.

We have remarked on some striking respects in which the conditions that undermine the voluntariness of action have counterparts affecting what may be termed in an extended sense the "voluntariness" of belief. But can we develop anything like a straightforward criterion of "weakly voluntary belief?" I would think so, if we exploit the evident connection between epistemic virtue, or, better, the possibility of a virtuously formed belief and the absence of these kinds of disabling conditions. My proposal is this.

> A belief is weakly voluntary to the extent that it is formed or held under circumstances (a) allowing for, but not dictating, its epistemically virtuous formation or retention; and that (b) had the subject not been epistemically virtuous, this belief would not have been held, or continued to be held, with the same degree of conviction.

Let me comment on some important features of this characterization.

First, on the notion of a "circumstance." Circumstances, as we discussed in section 4.1, can act to prompt or inhibit one's capacity to form beliefs on a virtuous basis. Where circumstances do play this prompting role, I will assume that circumstances allow, but do not "dictate," one's being virtuous. The notion of circumstances that "dictate virtue" I would leave to cover unusual cases where, somehow, one was *forced* to have an epistemically virtuous attitude.

Second, we must recall in this connection the important difference between one's making virtuous *efforts* and one's succeeding in exemplifying something like true epistemic virtue. Should this criterion be understood as requiring that circumstances permit virtuous efforts (merely) or as requiring that circumstances permit one's actually *being* epistemically virtuous? Many situations will certainly allow for virtuous efforts but with no possibility of success, owing to unconscious biases or other factors. Such factors—such biases and other influences—certainly deserve to be treated as undermining doxastic voluntariness. Hence, intuition would seem to favor the wider interpretation of "circumstances." Voluntary belief requires that circumstances permit one not only to try but to succeed in being epistemically virtuous.

Third, we need to notice, especially in reference to clause (b), that the above criterion concerns the (weak) voluntariness of a *belief*, rather than that of the person forming the belief. This becomes relevant whenever—as may certainly happen—an agent is able to exert certain virtuous efforts, but ones that have little or nothing to do with the actual determination of the belief in question. In such cases, I count the belief as *involuntary*. We may say that here the agent's *virtue* was voluntarily exerted, but this is not the same thing as the voluntariness of his belief itself.

We can observe now the operation of these considerations and our parent criterion in terms of the cases already enumerated. First, if a belief is the result of another's coercive efforts, to that extent it will not be, and in many instances will be such that it could not have been, the result of one's conscientious efforts. Thus, should a belief of mine have been triggered by post-hypnotic suggestion, then, even if I thought that it had resulted from virtuous efforts on my part, it has not. To be sure, the fact that this belief has resulted from something other than virtuous efforts does not by itself imply that it could not have been virtuously formed, but that is not the point. The point is that the nature of the processes from which the belief did result are reasonably construed as ruling out the possibility of virtuous determination. If the belief had been planted sufficiently firmly by hypnotic suggestion, then it would be true that epistemically virtuous efforts would have had no effect. Such a case, then, well illustrates our third comment regarding the difference between circumstances allowing one to exhibit epistemic virtue and circumstances allowing the virtuous formation of a given belief.

Certainly, too, afflictions that impair the functioning of one's cognitive system, depending on their severity, can have essentially the same effect. The circumstances in question will be such not only as to have usurped any constructive role for conscientious efforts, but also the possibility of their success.

Next consider the case of Terri. Terri's beliefs, it should be recalled, are motivated by genuinely conscientious desires, but circumstances prevent her from satisfactorily *realizing* these desires. Are her beliefs weakly voluntary? The answer is that they are somewhat so, although less voluntary than they would be if circumstances allowed her genuine conscientiousness to play a more significant role in the actual formation of these beliefs. Put otherwise, these circumstances do not inhibit Terri from making conscientious efforts, but they do prevent her beliefs from adequately reflecting these efforts. Hence, to this extent her beliefs remain (weakly) involuntary.

The case, however, of James at the Tobacco Institute is perhaps somewhat less clear-cut. His beliefs have not been the issuance of anything like virtuous efforts on his part, but this, he may plead, is the fault of circumstances and not of himself or of his epistemic character. Others, however, may point out that it is his own vices (say, a lack of independence of mind, a lack of what I call "intellectual courage") that are responsible for this failure of virtue. For his part, James may plead that if he lacked a certain independence of mind, this was not a vice whose operation was subject to his control; he may say that he was *trying* reasonably hard, and that if he was lacking in such independence of mind, this was the fault of the circumstances and not something that betokened anything like a culpable failure on his part. So here there is not, I think, a definite verdict.

Finally, let me address in this connection an important objection, which would seem to strike at the heart of any notion of doxastic voluntariness, especially as we have characterized it. H. H. Price (1954) observes that, at least under fairly optimal reflective conditions, it may seem that belief is voluntary. It may seem that we may allow that a person has voluntarily or freely opted for what seems most rational to her. But Price replies that

> this appearance is deceptive. It is not a free choice at all, but a
> forced one. If you are in a reasonable frame of mind, you cannot

help preferring the proposition which the evidence favors, much as
you may wish you could. (p. 16)

Why speak of voluntariness at all, if indeed one is "forced" even
under the best of circumstances to adopt the most reasonable proposition, given the evidence?

First, I would reply that this argument proves too much. One
might as well say that an agent in a suitably rational frame of mind
cannot but select the act that strikes him or her at the time as "most
rational." Surely, it should not follow from this that none of our
actions are voluntary. Perhaps the main point here could be put
more forcefully in this way. The claim that an agent in a suitably
rational frame of mind must accept the most rational, or apparently
most rational, conclusion of a given bit of evidence masks more
than it reveals. For if by a "rational frame of mind" one means
anything like what I would call an epistemically *virtuous* frame of
mind, treating the former as a mere given, serves but to fix what I
have maintained is a crucial *variable* subject to one's control. Thus,
as I will want to maintain, on many occasions persons are subject
to doxastic blame or fault precisely because they have not applied
themselves in such a way as to be in a Pricean "rational frame of
mind." Price, then, has not succeeded in refuting a notion of what
I would call weakly voluntary belief.

2. Strong Doxastic Voluntarism

Still, in part for reasons brought out in our initial discussion in this
chapter, I agree that one should not be entirely happy with calling
"weakly voluntary" beliefs *fully* voluntary. Such beliefs, although
they do not go against one's will, appear to lack voluntariness in
that they are not truly *subject* to one's will. They are, or can be,
the product of one's relatively unbothered thought—of one's virtuous response to the evidence bearing on the belief in question—
but not one's will or desires. To this extent, whereas voluntary action
involves "doing what one would like" (under the circumstances),
weakly voluntary belief does not involve "believing what one would
like." At best or at most, it seems to involve believing what one
ought from an epistemic standpoint.

I begin this discussion, though, by considering a type of case in
which a stronger notion of doxastic voluntarism appears to be exhibited. Take the following item (from the philosophical annals of

my current home state, Tennessee). Bubba is a man of limited education and intellectual sophistication (but he is not stupid). Bubba's son, Billy Bob, has been accused of murder and considerable evidence of his son's guilt has been presented. Yet, for understandable reasons, Bubba refuses to admit his son's guilt and insists on believing in his son's innocence. Bubba admits that the evidence apparently stands very much in favor of his son's guilt and that it certainly does not favor his son's innocence; still, he refuses, he says, to allow himself to be swayed by this. Under these circumstances, is it not correct to say that Bubba voluntarily believes that Billy Bob is innocent (not guilty)?

Before proceeding, I will try to address another objection of Price's (1954, pp. 17, 21–22) because this one threatens to undercut any voluntarist interpretation of Bubba's case. Price holds that such apparently voluntaristic locutions as "I refuse to belief that *x*" indicate not a successful application of willpower, but instead a determination to *bring about* a hoped-for state of affairs. Thus, for Price, when Bubba refuses to believe that Billy Bob is guilty, this merely indicates a determination on Bubba's part to bring it about that he does not have this belief, by such appropriate actions as focusing on the evidence that he is innocent (say, the good things he has done, the times he helped his mother, and so forth).

I disagree with any such analysis. For it seems that, most often, we take it that a person who says "I refuse to believe that" *already* does not believe the item in question, thus, is not prepared merely at some *later* time to rid himself of that belief. That is why the claim, "I refuse to believe that, but, alas, I do believe it" is at best a curious joke, not a legitimate possibility uncovered by sound philosophical analysis. (Likewise, for the person who says, "I insist on believing that, but unfortunately I don't believe it.")

The obvious reason, then, to think of Bubba's apparent belief in his son's innocence as voluntary is it reflects Bubba's *will* (i.e., his determination to believe just that thing). But it does not merely reflect such determination. That determination is itself rooted, no doubt, in certain relevant desires on Bubba's part. He does not *want* his son to be, or to have been, guilty, nor does he want to believe that his son is guilty.

Mere causation by one's desires, though, even causation by a specific desire to believe that *p*, is not enough to make a belief that *p* strongly voluntary. Otherwise, beliefs due simply to unconscious wishful thinking would qualify as voluntary, which they are not. If mere wishful thinking were to unconsciously work its effect on Bubba, if Bubba *thought* that his son were plainly innocent, thought that the evidence plainly showed this, and were entirely unaware of the effect that his desire had had on his evaluation of the evidence, Bubba would just be deluded. Bubba's belief would be anything but voluntary. (In fact, arguably it would not even qualify as weakly voluntary.)

What is crucial, then, to the voluntariness of this belief is that Bubba be aware of this determination and at least have some cognizance—though this is a subtle matter—of its influence on his belief. Certainly, Bubba cannot be under the false impression that his determination has had *no* influence on what he believes. But, at the same time, in affirming his son's innocence, it does not seem that Bubba could have a vivid, concurrent awareness that he believes this simply because he wants to.[4]

At this point, then, let me propose for purposes of discussion the following characterization of "strongly voluntary belief":

> A belief is strongly voluntary just in case (a) it originates in part as a result of the subject's determination to believe that thing and (b) the subject is aware (to some extent) of this determination of and its effect on his belief.

Conditions (a) and (b), I want to say, are both necessary for strongly voluntary belief, but are they sufficient?

One may doubt the voluntariness of Bubba's belief on the following grounds:[5] Is this a belief that he has *voluntarily chosen*, or is this a belief he merely finds himself with, given his strong desires? For instance, could he have avoided forming this belief? Bubba, it may be said, is just a guy with a very *strong* disposition to think his son innocent of *any* (serious) charge that might come his way. He has no more chosen this belief, or arrived at it voluntarily, than he has chosen any other strong doxastic disposition, such as his tendency to think ill of strangers.

In reply to this fairly persuasive point, however, the defender of strong doxastic voluntarism may wish to change the case slightly. Thus take Carl, Bubba's educated younger brother. Carl, too, is instinctively drawn to rejecting the evidence against Billy Bob. Yet he is honest enough to admit to himself that this evidence is strong; it is by sheer determination that he overcomes this instinct, overcomes all contrary temptation, and allows himself to follow the evidence. Is that not a clear instance of strongly voluntary belief?

Yet there are problems even with this case. For one, take the problem of *incentives*, which is relevant not only to Carl's but to Bubba's case as well. The idea is this. If either Bubba or Carl did not originally respond to the evidence by believing Billy Bob innocent, there is no (nonevidentiary) factor, no special incentives that would change either of their minds (cf. Bennett [1990, p. 88]). This is not to say that such incentives as money cannot change a person's beliefs. But they can do so only over time or by exerting an unconscious effect. One cannot choose to believe for the sake, say, of a monetary incentive in the same way that one can choose to act simply for the sake of such an incentive. And that, it may be held, is a signal indicator of the fact that belief is not directly responsive to practical considerations—to considerations of practical reason.

This conclusion, notice, agrees nicely with our earlier discussion of the difference between reasons for thinking true and reasons for getting oneself to think something true (section 3.2). The ultimate point in both cases is the same. Practical reasons, or what are perceived as such, do not directly influence belief in a conscious way, but do so only by way of influencing one to act in such a way as to affect belief. It is epistemic reasons—reasons pertaining to the truth or falsity of the particular belief content in question—that are susceptible of direct (conscious) influence on belief.[6]

Return now to Carl's case. What I want to say is mainly that Carl's belief is *weakly* voluntary: the kind of willpower described here is really nothing more than ordinary conscientiousness (epistemic virtue) applied to the specific case of fighting off a temptation. In this regard, it is no different from conscientiousness applied, say, to the task of fighting off a tendency to racial bias. What Carl is doing is simply exerting himself, as best he can, to be guided by the evidence and not by personal biases. In this regard, he certainly exhibits admirable epistemic virtue—again, his belief exhibits weak voluntariness but not strong voluntariness. Why not? Because there is a difference between such conscientious exertions and believing as a result of desiring to believe a certain content. Carl does not desire to believe that his nephew is guilty. On the contrary, presumably he desires to believe him innocent. And whereas it is true to describe Carl's belief as influenced by his conscientious desire to believe what is true, this would characterize any epistemically conscientious belief or action. It is not, by any means, sufficient for strongly voluntary belief.

One last point, but an important one. It is notable that only *weak* voluntariness is required for the judgments of doxastic and moral responsibility that ultimately concern me. Strong voluntariness, in this regard, turns out to be essentially unimportant, or at least unnecessary. Take the case of Bubba and Billy Bob. Bubba may be judged doxastically culpable for his belief, but even if this belief were not strongly voluntary (even were it the product merely of wishful thinking), it could *still* qualify as culpable. Nor would I be inclined to say that wishful thinking, in general, is any better or less culpable a practice than believing as a result of a conscious determination to believe some given thing. At least the person guilty of strongly voluntary belief has some appreciation of the general direction of the evidence, an appreciation that would betoken what is an epistemically desirable habit, even if it is one that is occasionally overridden by very strong desires. By way of contrast, wishful thinking itself tends to be habitual and of course a bad habit at that. So the contrast here is between a destructive habit (from an epistemic standpoint) and a basically sound habit that occasionally gets overridden by exceptionally strong desires. (Interestingly, "wishful thinker" names a personality type; "willful believer" does not—or at least does not to nearly the same extent.)

3. Acceptance, Assent, and Belief

The present study defends the eminent suitability of *belief* as a subject of responsibility and normative evaluation generally. However, one finds in some of the more recent literature a notion of "acceptance" or "assent" that bids fair to replace belief as a proper subject of normative epistemic scrutiny, because it has been thought *voluntary* in a way in which belief is not. Here I want to devote some attention to these accounts, first, by way of characterizing this notion, or these notions (of acceptance and assent), and, second, by way of examining their credentials regarding voluntariness.

✳   ✳   ✳

The first and arguably most prominent characteristic of the relevant notions of "acceptance" or "assent" is its truth-oriented *motivation*. These are acts of acceptance or assent, which are (or which would be) motivated by a desire to hold true beliefs and not by wishful thinking or any other epistemically irresponsible desire. Thus Keith Lehrer (1981) speaks of accepting a proposition "in the interest of truth":

[I]f someone tells me something surprising but extremely unpleasant and I know that he is utterly reliable, I may find that I cannot quite believe what he says, but I can accept what he says. . . . We may be unable to alter confidence immediately in the face of new evidence. But we can accept in the interest of truth what we cannot yet fully believe. (p. 79)

Mark Kaplan's (1981) notion of acceptance is similar in this regard. He stipulates

X accepts p is just shorthand for "X would defend P were her sole aim to defend the truth". (p. 138)

Compare here as well the notion of "assent" developed by Ronald De Sousa (1971). On De Sousa's account, belief itself is a disposition, a disposition whose definitive exercise is an act of "assent," which he characterizes as follows. We make assertions, he says,

for any number of reasons. . . . But insofar as assertion is sincere or candid we can abstract from it a bet on the truth alone, solely determined by epistemic desirabilities. Such an act, or such an abstraction, I shall term Assent. (p. 59, emphasis suppressed)

Second, this postulated act of truth-oriented acceptance is conceived by its advocates as *qualitative* as opposed to something like a Bayesian "degree of confidence." It is conceived as a flat-out acceptance of or assent to a given proposition. Such assent may be accompanied by a greater or lesser degree of confidence; moreover, the proposition to which assent has thus been given may itself express some estimation of a probability. But even in such cases as the latter, a distinction remains between the proposition to which assent is flat-out given and one's degree of confidence in the truth of this proposition. (See in this regard, Kaplan [1981, p. 135] and De Sousa [1971, pp. 58–59].)

Third, acceptance or assent is typically conceived of as distinguishable in some way from belief. For instance, this distinction is drawn in terms of the difference between belief as a *disposition* and acceptance or assent as *acts*. L. Jonathan Cohen (1989) offers perhaps the clearest illustration of this tendency. For Cohen, acceptance that *p* is an act whereby one chooses "to have or adopt a policy of deeming, positing or postulating that *p*" (p. 368), a policy that one may adopt for any number of reasons ranging from purely practical concerns to considerations of truth and evidence. Such a decision, Cohen says, is different from belief that *p*, which is a *disposition* "to feel that it is true that *p*" (p. 368). Likewise, De Sousa (1971) casts this difference as one between disposition and act, although making the connection between the two quite close. Although "belief proper," De Sousa insists, is a disposition, it is a disposition whose "privileged" and distinctive expression is an act of assent.

> Assent to p by X either serves to incorporate p, or shows that p is already incorporated in the set of sentences taken by X to be true. Such inclusion constitutes the necessary and sufficient condition for X to believe that p. (p. 59)

There is, however, another reason why acceptance and assent may be distinguished from belief. A person may, as in the case previously cited by Lehrer,[7] accept *p* without having any corresponding belief that *p* because acceptance, insofar as it is "in the interest of truth" may differ from one's belief dispositions, which may be dictated by other concerns.

Fourth, there is the allegedly *voluntary* character of acceptance—in comparison to belief. Cohen (1989) is very explicit on this point. Acceptance, he says, "occurs at will because at bottom it executes a choice—the accepter's choice of which propositions to take as his premises" (p. 370). Whereas acceptance is thus voluntary, belief is not; with belief, it is simply a matter of discovering what one is disposed to think. Lehrer's (1981) view on this point, moreover, seems quite the same as Cohen's. One "primary difference," Lehrer says, between acceptance and belief "is the element of optionality." Sometimes, he continues, "a person cannot decide what to believe, but he can decide what to accept" (p. 79). De Sousa (1971), on this point, seems largely to agree with Lehrer and Cohen. Assent, he says, is a voluntary action—even though, he admits, the character of the motives ("epistemic wants" [p. 60]) determining this action are such as normally to be the cause only of these acts of assent and not any other kind of action. (Thus, he concedes, assent is not accompanied by an ability to do otherwise.) Kaplan (1981) speaks in similarly voluntaristic terms. In distinguishing acceptance from a Bayesian "degree of confidence," for instance, he appeals to the Popperian recommendation that one sometimes takes high *risks* to arrive at comprehensive theories, even ones that, one fears, are likely to be false (cf. p. 139). Evidently, this is a voluntary strategy.

✳ ✳ ✳

What do I find objectionable in such doctrines? Where belief *is* truth-motivated and thus rather less clearly distinguishable from acceptance or assent, I see relatively less to take issue with, but even here there is one problem. If we allow that belief is a dispositional notion, I would think that we would want to grant the same status to acceptance and recognize that it is *assent* that is different in this regard. Thus, talk of what I accept is basically talk of what I have or *would* assent to; in this respect it is no different from belief. By contrast, talk of what I "assent to" does not seem to be merely dispositional. Even if it is true that by assenting to *p* I may thereby ("tacitly") assent to other propositions I am not explicitly considering, this does not show that assent is dispositional but only that its reach extends beyond the explicit limits of what one is currently considering. (Compare "I've accepted that proposition for years" and "I've assented to that proposition for years." Clearly it is more natural to use the former in reference to a merely continuous state and the latter in reference, say, to periodic affirmations when queried.)

The more revealing situation, though, is when belief is *not* truth-motivated, for now deeper differences emerge between belief and both acceptance and assent. Thus consider any prima facie case of what I have called "strongly voluntary belief." For example, suppose that I have just been presented with some extremely strong evidence that Jones, my financial adviser and someone whom I took to be a very good friend, has been stealing from me for years. I am shocked by the presentation; yet I recover my composure enough to reply sincerely that "I just refuse to believe that Jones is a thief." In fact, I announce, again sincerely, that

(1) I continue to believe that Jones is an honest man.

This belief would qualify as strongly voluntary in the same way, and to the same extent, as Bubba's. But, for the moment, we need only insist on one point: that I do genuinely believe that Jones is an honest man. The question to be addressed first here is what my *motivation* for believing it happens to be. Do I accept this honesty in the interest of *truth*? Well, notice in this regard that I might concede that a purely objective observer (which I admit that I am not) viewing the evidence, would find it very unlikely that Jones is innocent. I might affirm, that is to say, and let us suppose that I do affirm, something like the following.

(2) If I were an entirely objective observer whose interests in this matter were entirely those of truth, then I would find it unlikely that Jones is innocent.

Evidently, then, I do not in any straightforward way accept Jones's innocence in the "interest of truth" or "out of a desire for true beliefs," or with the (predominant) "aim of defending the truth." Of course, I do think that the proposition affirming Jones's innocence is true, but I do not think this *out* of any particularly truth-oriented motivation. To this extent, I do not accept or assent to this proposition (in the relevant sense distinguished by Lehrer, De Sousa, and Kaplan); I merely believe it.

It is notable, then, that in the present case, the postulated association between acceptance and voluntariness breaks down. Here, evidently, it is my belief in Jones's innocence (the expression of my determination to believe in that innocence) that, regardless of the possibility of "strongly voluntary belief," surely qualifies as *more* voluntary than anything I might concede regarding the state of the evidence for *p*. Grudgingly, I may accept the unlikelihood of Jones's innocence (given the evidence), while keeping my conviction that he is innocent.

Or consider a different version of this case. This time I am an epistemically scrupulous sort who really does want to believe in accordance with the evidence, which I do recognize as enough to reasonably establish Jones's guilt. Yet, as Lehrer puts it, I "cannot quite believe" that Jones is a thief. My belief disposition is, one might say, "recalcitrant." Now this case is different in at least one important respect. In this case, it is what I accept in the interest of truth, rather than what I believe, which lays the better claim to voluntariness. In this case, my belief that Jones is innocent is not the product of anything like a conscious determination to believe or to continue believing that. Still, it is not clear that we need recognize any special state of truth-motivated acceptance here either; for even though I do not believe that Jones is guilty, I do have a belief that would seem a perfectly adequate surrogate for a truth-motivated act of assent: namely, a belief to the effect that the *evidence* is sufficient for Jones's guilt.

Is the latter belief, though, voluntary in the way that my truth-motivated acceptance of his guilt is supposed to be? Certainly, unlike my recalcitrant belief in Jones's guilt, this belief is not contrary to my will; and certainly unlike my belief in Jones's innocence (in the first version of this story), it is not the product of my will. In fact, given fairly natural assumptions about the background of this case, it seems clear that this belief would qualify, in terms of our previous standard, as "weakly voluntary." But the main point is just this. There is no apparent difference between the extent to which I am free to accept (in the interest of truth) the judgment that Jones is guilty and the extent to which I am free to accept and believe that the evidence supports this conclusion. I cannot very well say that "I accept in the interest of truth that he is guilty, but I cannot quite believe that the evidence supports this." Nor, conversely, can I say that "I cannot accept in the interest of truth that he is guilty, although I do believe that there is adequate evidence that he is."

One final query. Might we need a notion of assent or acceptance for some purpose other than its alleged voluntariness? Kaplan's ultimate interest is in a conception of *rational* acceptance. Interestingly, he is able to show that rational acceptance cannot be conceived as "rational degree of confidence." I dispute the claim, though, that rational acceptance can be conceived in terms of his notion of acceptance (as what one would defend were one's sole aim to defend the truth). The difficulty, simply put, is that if I irrationally defend something like Jones's innocence *not* out of any aim of defending the truth, but for other, personal motives, apparently I do not (by Kaplan's lights) accept the proposition at all. But in that case, instead of being able to criticize me for irrational acceptance, we are, with some embarrassment, forced to conclude that I do not accept the proposition at all. Of course, Kaplan might reply that as long as you believe that Jones is innocent (whatever your underlying motivation), you regard this proposition as *true* and, thus, in defending it, are acting with the aim of defending the truth. But if that is how x-ing "with the aim of defending the truth" is to be understood, belief that p becomes necessary and sufficient for acceptance that p. So what, then, becomes the point of introducing the notion of acceptance in the first place? Evidently, there is only a *difference* between belief and acceptance if x-ing "with the aim of defending the truth" refers to one's *motivation* in defending p, rather than to whether or not one believes that p is true.

Notes

1. Perhaps the best-known contemporary statement of the involuntarist position is Bernard Williams (1973), but also see the examples enumerated in chapter 1, note 1.

2. Some of these claims, regarding the analogous roles played by reasons for action (in the case of action) and reason for thinking true (in the case of belief) are developed more extensively in my (1986).

3. Robert Kane (1985) is very good on this point. Kane emphasizes in his account of free will the importance of value incommensurabilities and value "experiments."

4. Nicholas Wolterstorff (1991, p. 123) makes the interesting suggestion that in such cases the subject would recognize that he *believes* out of his will (or desire) to believe, but that he would not think that the proposition in question is *true* in virtue of such desire. Thus, Bubba would say that "I believe that he is innocent mainly because I want to believe this; but I don't think that he is innocent because I want to believe him innocent." However, there is still an obvious tension here which Wolterstorff does not attempt in any way to alleviate. If I say that, on my view, proposition *p* is true in virtue of state of affairs *p* obtaining in the world, that would certainly suggest that I regard myself as believing *p* on grounds *other than* a desire to believe *p*.

5. Here, and at other places in the discussion to follow, I have been greatly helped by my conversations with Crispin Sartwell.

6. It may be noted that if this analysis is correct, the sense in which there are "innocent beliefs"—cf. Heil (1984) and Mele (1986)—is quite different from the sense in which there are actions that exhibit weakness of will. In the latter, I directly choose to do what I recognize to be wrong (or supported by weaker practical reasons); but in the former I do not directly choose to believe that which I regard as having less reason to think true than some incompatible belief.

7. Lehrer (1990, p. 11), I should point out, has allowed that acceptance in the interest of truth is a kind of belief.

Chapter Six

Epistemic Virtue and Justification

We have explored in the preceding discussion the interconnected notions of epistemic conscientiousness, virtue, responsibility, and voluntariness. Now is the time, however, to look at the "bigger picture." How does this view of belief and our responsibility for belief comport with the broader subject matter of epistemology? How, for that matter, does it comport with the even broader subject matter of the normative disciplines—taking epistemology and ethics as the latter's main constituents?

1. Character and Normative Judgment

The epistemological account to be proposed here links what I take to be a fundamental term of epistemic evaluation—one's being (subjectively) *justified* in forming (or having) a certain belief and one's epistemic character, insofar as this is reflected in the relevant processes by which one has either acquired or continued to have that belief. I begin, though, with a somewhat broader discussion of how and why personal qualities (the virtues and vices, both moral and epistemic) should enter into the normative judgments we make concerning persons' actions and beliefs. In particular, I begin with some reflections on this subject—or an aspect of this subject— drawn from David Hume's moral philosophy.[1]

One of Hume's most familiar doctrines pertains to the role of judgments of personal character in relation to moral judgments regarding persons' actions. On this view of Hume, whereas moral judgments are recognized as typically directed on actions, the idea is that we are concerned to make these judgments only to the extent that actions manifest recognizable personal traits, traits of moral *character*. Thus, for Hume, we call an act "vicious" or "wrong" or "immoral" insofar as its performance on a particular occasion, or perhaps its typical performance ranging over many occasions, manifests, or is liable to manifest, some personal demerit like greed or ingratitude.

Hume gives basically two reasons for this focus on character. First, from the standpoint of the person *making* the moral judgment, it is qualities of character that excite our interest fundamentally because it is *personal* qualities, and not actions per se, that ultimately interest us. As persons, it is hardly surprising that it should be these deep qualities of persons that most concern us. Acts, intentions, even particular motives excite our moral praise or blame insofar as they display something more abiding and more "personal": what we call moral character. Likewise, from the standpoint of the person *being* judged, insofar as we are passing judgment on that person, we need something more substantial, more abiding than a mere act or thought. After all, it is not the thought or the motive that we ultimately judge to be culpable—it is the person. If we are to indict or praise a person, the thought is that we must find something that is genuinely, and not just haphazardly or temporarily, associated with him, and this would be some feature of his moral character. (It is not, then, character traits as such that interest us, but character traits insofar as these are truly abiding states of a person.)

Let me put the point in this way in reference now to epistemology and belief rather than to ethics and action. Hume's insight, or its implication for my epistemological interests, is that a normative approach to epistemology is not distinctive simply in invoking notions of praise and blame, of responsibility and culpability, but that it is distinctive in a second regard. A normative judgment, epistemic or moral, latches onto certain features of *persons*: that is our primary interest. But that means that it latches onto epistemic activity insofar as this manifests recognizable traits of personal character. Whereas it is possible to discern and discuss all sorts of purely abstract relations of beliefs—relations of deductive and inductive logic—insofar as our concerns are truly normative in anything *like* a moral sense, the Humean point would be that we must go beyond these relations and discern whatever personal qualities may in any given instance underlie them.

2. Virtue and Justification

Let us turn from these general reflections regarding the evaluation of persons to the particular form of normative appraisal that has received the most attention in contemporary epistemology: namely, epistemic *justification*. Now, we have already encountered and very briefly criticized (section 1.2) two leading types of contemporary approaches to epistemic justification (the externalist and internalist), but our focus there was on these views as providing a basis for one's moral culpability. We shall return to such criticisms in section 6.3. But for the moment, let us adopt a more positive stance, as there is an alternative standard of justification already suggested by our discussion to this point. I shall simply offer this standard, and then attempt to shape and clarify it in response to certain difficulties it faces:

> *S* is justified in believing *p* insofar as *S* is epistemically virtuous in believing *p*.

The first such difficulty concerns the status, on this view, of spontaneous perceptual beliefs—and other reliable modes of belief acquisition that typically occur under circumstances not allowing for virtuous (or unvirtuous) efforts. Are these all to be treated as unjustified beliefs, and in that case what becomes of other beliefs seemingly justified on the basis of these? I answer in three comments:

(a) First, I should say that I want to treat spontaneous perceptual beliefs—and other such beliefs as occur under conditions not allowing for virtuous efforts—as neither justified nor unjustified. I want to treat "justified" and "unjustified," in other words, as contraries rather than as contradictories, matching in this regard the relation between virtue and vice. Between these contrary poles lie beliefs, such as spontaneous perceptual beliefs, which are properly classed as "excusable." Having them reflects no credit, or, for the same reason, no discredit on one. These are simply a kind of automatic response to one's external or internal environment.

(b) My second point here reiterates what was said in the discussion of perceptual beliefs at section 4.3. Even where a belief's original acquisition (and later history, at least for a time) do not allow of virtuous efforts, its *use* at some suitable time may qualify as highly virtuous or unvirtuous. Now, the use of a belief may refer to the circumstance of one's acting on that belief, but in this connection the use that interests us is in *inference*. Thus, perceptual beliefs that are originally neither justified nor unjustified may be virtuously or unvirtuously used to arrive at other beliefs, in which case one will be justified, or unjustified, in having those other beliefs. They will be justified by one's perceptual belief in the sense that one has virtuously used the latter to arrive at the former.

(c) Notice, I did not speak in the preceding discussion of an originally unjustified perception as justifying some inferential belief. Rather, I spoke of a justified *use* of the former. On this notion of epistemic justification, then, what renders the inferred belief justified is *not* the propositional content of the original perceptual belief. Rather, it is a quality pertaining to the activity of using this received content. So, for example, if I glimpse what looks like a spotted owl, I become justified in the reflective conviction that it is a spotted owl to the extent that I have exhibited due care in my examination of that original impression or series of impressions.

Let us move on to a second and related area of concern—spotlighted by such cases as this. Suppose that John and Jim are both avidly investigating whether a given item *p* is true. Surely it could *happen* that whereas both find information sufficient to convince them that *p*, John's information turns out to be much better than Jim's. Objectively speaking, it provides better support for the belief that *p* and, to that extent, it provides John with a better justification than has Jim. Yet, it may also be that both are equally virtuous in their beliefs.

This is an important difficulty requiring that we make an important distinction. One fair attempt at this distinction (see, for instance, the excellent discussion of this in Kvanvig [1992]) would go as follows. In this case, it may be helpful to say that John's *belief* enjoys a justification that is superior to that enjoyed by Jim's but also to say that both *persons* are to be judged or evaluated as equally entitled to have, or as equally justified in having, these beliefs. Thus one distinguishes, or attempts to distinguish, a belief's enjoying a certain justification from a person's being justified in having that belief. Moreover, we can easily relate this distinction to the foregoing discussion of perception and perceptual justification. Personal justification will relate to the quality of a person's use of such things as perceptually acquired information. Depending on the quality of effort, the *person* will be justified or not justified in holding to the inferred belief. At the same time, a *belief's* justification may be naturally construed as dependent on its relation (as a belief *content*) to other belief contents.

Having introduced a terminology for distinguishing two modes of epistemic justification, let me now introduce what I regard as a somewhat happier, but equivalent, terminology. I shall speak—instead of a "person's being justified"—of a person's being *subjec-*

tively justified in having a certain belief and—instead of a "belief's being justified"—of its being *objectively justified* (for that person). Why this preference? I do not think that mere talk of persons and beliefs being justified bears, or should be made to bear, very much philosophical weight. After all, it seems hard to argue against the simple thesis that a person is justified in believing a given content if and only if that content is justified (for that person at that time); in other words, it is not clear that the two ways of speaking are not, in some sense, equivalent (cf. Kvanvig [1992, p. 71ff]). Still, I want to insist that talk of persons' and beliefs' having justification does in this connection *point* to an important difference, which may be expressed in familiar philosophical terms as a difference between "subjective" and "objective" justification. Beyond their familiarity, these terms have the advantage of conveying quite well the intended difference between justification as reflecting a person's optimal use of his own resources versus justification as something impersonal, something that depends (at least in part) on objectively definable relations holding among belief contents or between these and objective features of one's epistemic situation (e.g., facts about how a belief was acquired and the reliability of this mode of acquisition under these circumstances).[2]

Later, we shall have to defend this notion of subjective justification by way of giving some positive motivation for our view. First, though, I shall attempt to defend it against some possible criticisms emanating from philosophically hostile voices to be found in the recent literature on epistemic justification.

Alvin Goldman (1980, section V) has argued, as follows, against any notion of subjective epistemic justification. Beginning with the seemingly analogous case of moral justification, Goldman points out that subjective *moral* justification may be with some initial plausibility captured in either of two ways:

(a) *S* is subjectively justified in doing *x* if and only if *S* believes that he is morally justified in doing *x*.

(b) *S* is subjectively justified in doing *x* if and only if *S* justifiably believes that he is morally justified in doing *x*.

These, he maintains, have the following equivalents for subjective epistemic justification:

(a)' *S* is subjectively justified in believing *p* if and only if *S* believes that he is (objectively) justified in believing *p*.

(b)' *S* is subjectively justified in believing *p* if and only if *S* (objectively) justifiably believes that he is (objectively) justified in believing that *p*.

But (a)' is objectionable on the same grounds as (a): it is too permissive. Subjective justification ought to be more than only thinking yourself justified, especially if it is to be used to excuse otherwise bad conduct that is based on it. In the case of ethical justification, this type of consideration, then, mandates a move from (a) to (b) and, thus, one might think, from (a)' to (b)'. But (b)'—if we correctly insist that both uses of "justified" are objective, so as to avoid circularity—hardly seems to capture a notion of *subjective* justification at all.

However, there is a ready reply to this. I would want to place the same requirement on "thinking oneself objectively justified" that I have placed on a person's being (subjectively) justified in believing that *p*—that is to say: the account proposed earlier in terms of epistemic virtue. Notice, if we do that, "subjective justification" turns out to be less permissive than merely "believing oneself (objectively) justified" because it involves constraints of epistemic virtue—but it remains, equally obviously, distinct from any notion of objective justification.

I move now to a different theorist, William P. Alston. Now a characteristic of subjective justification (at least as I conceive it) is that under many circumstances (those described in chapter 4) we may be held responsible for our failures to be epistemically justified in our beliefs. This, however, will certainly require that under those circumstances it is possible for us to determine by some appropriate amount of reflection *whether* or not we are epistemically justified. If, for instance (in line with the entire argument of section 1.2), I am to be held culpable for some action insofar as this action was grounded in some culpable belief of mine, we must surely allow that it was possible for me to determine, then or at some earlier time, by suitable reflection that this belief was not virtuously held (i.e., was not subjectively justified). Alston, however, has raised a number of interesting difficulties for any such claim.

I will break into Alston's (1986) discussion at the point at which he is considering a notion of epistemic justification that, if it is not exactly the same as ours, bears some important and enlightening similarities to ours. The view is this:

S is justified in believing that p if and only if S's belief that p did not, so far as S can tell, stem from S's violations of intellectual obligations. (p. 208)

Alston writes in refutation of this revised criterion, however:

> We rarely have reason to think that one of our beliefs stems from
> intellectual transgressions. To know about the causal history of our
> beliefs takes research, and we rarely engage in such research. Hence
> we have very few beliefs about the causal history of our beliefs.
> And so practically all beliefs, no matter how shoddy or disreputable,
> will be justified on this criterion. (p. 208)

Applied to the case of subjective justification, this would mean that
we would almost always be subjectively justified in our beliefs (that
presumably even Hitler would be subjectively justified in his beliefs), for we would seldom, if ever, be able to determine that their
genesis reflected some culpable shortfall in epistemic virtue (my
equivalent for a violation of what Alston calls our "intellectual
obligations").

However, I would reply as follows. Dan the dogmatist may rarely
engage in research on, or think much about, "the causal history of
his beliefs" but, assuming that many of these beliefs *do* issue from
intellectual transgressions or from a lack of acceptably virtuous
efforts it may well be true that Dan *has* ample reason to think that
this is so. Basically, this same point came up in chapter 4 (section
4.1). Recall that a person's own lack of epistemic virtue leads him
not to *recognize* that a particular situation calls for some special
virtuous efforts is not necessarily a valid excuse. It does not mean
that such recognition was not possible. Alston, then, may be correct to suppose as a psychological fact that we rarely think that our
beliefs result from intellectual transgressions, but it does not follow, as he wishes to suppose, that we rarely have *reason* to think
that this is so.

One last point by way of reinforcing these contentions. At least
on the account proposed here, nothing like a full examination of
the causal history of one's belief is required for epistemic justification. What is required is, rather, that if we are to blame a person
for believing that *p*, it must have been possible for her to determine that her belief was not virtuously held. This, admittedly, requires some scrutiny of one's current motives ("Is this wishful thinking or can I now say that I have really attempted to find the truth
about this matter?"), but it does not require anything like a full
examination of all of the factors which led to a belief's original
acquisition.

Alston, however, has more to say of considerable interest in this context. For he has attempted, more fundamentally, to attack the very notion that reflection is ever sufficient to determine whether or not one is epistemically justified. He writes:

> Consider the ethical analogy. . . . Often I have to engage in considerable research to determine whether a proposed action is justified. If it is a question of whether I would be justified in making a certain decision as department chairman, . . . I cannot ascertain this just by reflection, unless I have thoroughly internalized the various rules, regulations, by-laws, and so on. (1986, pp. 217–18)

I would reply as follows. Suppose that one has made a good-faith effort to consult what one takes to be the relevant materials for determining whether a given action (say, as department chair) is justified. Obviously, from an objective standpoint, one still may be incorrect in the sense that in virtue of other materials (materials unbeknown to one) this policy is not justified. Still, do we not, especially for purposes of praising and blaming, want to capture a notion of *subjective* justification according to which such good-faith efforts would justify one in belief and in action based on that belief? Moreover, whether one has made such good-faith efforts *is*—even allowing for self-deception and related psychological difficulties—often determinable based on reflection.[3]

3. Virtue and Justification (Continued)

We have to a certain extent defended the idea of subjective justification (couched in terms of epistemic virtue). But there remains the more basic question of why, positively, we need to employ the notion of epistemic virtue specifically as a view about *justification?* Why not—it may be asked—talk simply in terms of beliefs as virtuous or not and leave the troublesome term "justification" out of the discussion? What content do we *add* in insisting on talking about justification—if the kind of justification invoked by this criterion is so fundamentally at variance with its objective counterpart? Surely *knowledge* cannot begin to be true, justified belief in this sense of "justified." My response to such questions will be this. We need this notion of subjective epistemic justification because it is *this* notion of justification—and not any rival notion—that correctly matches our assessments of *moral justification*. It is this notion of epistemic justification—in preference to alternative internalist and externalist notions—that properly yields a basis, I shall try to show, for a conception of morally justified action. Let us see how this case can be made:

(i) From the perspective of externalism, it is quite possible for an individual to possess an adequate justification for believing *p*, yet, intuitively, this not be adequate to justify acting on *p*. For the externalist cheerfully allows that an individual might have a reliable belief-producing mechanism, say, some power of clairvoyance (cf. Bonjour [1980]), but a mechanism which it would be epistemically irresponsible for him to believe was reliable and thus morally irresponsible for him to act on. If this is not immediately clear, imagine that a certain boat owner (cf. Clifford [1877]) has, unbeknown to himself, an infallible power of detecting leaks. So far as he is aware, however, the boat should be full of leaks. The boat is not full of leaks, but, it seems clear, he would not be morally justified in sending persons off to sea in this boat. (Surely such a clairvoyant would be no more justified in thus sending people off than would be someone who had simply made a lucky guess that his boat had no fatal leaks.) Notice, too, that the externalist also has a problem in the *converse* circumstance. As we saw in connection with the Mary Smith case (section 1.2), a person can be, from an externalist standpoint, *un*justified in a certain belief, yet, intuitively, can be justified in acting on this belief.

(ii) Contrasting in this regard my own view and the *internalist* view is admittedly a trickier matter. However, begin with the case of a person who holds a justified belief—justified by internalist standards—yet out of unvirtuous motives. A teacher, say, paddles a student whom he thinks he has caught cheating. The teacher's evidence is sufficient to justify the verdict (that the student should be paddled), or so we shall suppose. Moreover, the teacher is actually moved by this evidence to consider the student guilty. However, underlying this conclusion is not any genuine desire to find out whether this student is guilty but simply an animosity toward the student. In other words, the teacher takes cognizance of and is affected by what is sufficient evidence, but what underlies his being moved by this evidence is not the recognition that this genuinely is sufficient evidence (that is not his concern), but his underlying animosity toward the student.

The case is somewhat subtle. But I want to have it that the beliefs that purport to justify the guilty verdict do serve as causes of the justified belief in the student's guilt. I want the argument which follows to cover both internalists who require and those who do not require the beliefs justifying a given belief to serve as causes of that belief (see chapter 1, note 6). Now what to say about such a case? For my intuitions, the right thing to say about such cases is clear. Neither the concrete, specific action of this teacher's paddling this student on this occasion nor the concrete, specific belief on which it is based is truly justified. To be sure, materials exist out of which a justification could have been *constructed* both for the act and the belief. But that is not the same thing. Quite likely, there are those, Jew and Gentile alike, who believe that the Holocaust was part of God's plan (perhaps that, without it, the modern state of Israel would have been impossible). In that sense, a justification could perhaps be "constructed" for the Holocaust. But that would hardly show that the perpetrators of these crimes were justified in their actions.

My conclusion, then, is this. Insofar as internalism allows the possibility of a justified but unvirtuously held belief, it does not provide an intuitive basis for an account of morally justified action. Even if we suppose, in other words, for purposes of discussion, that paddling can be morally justified under the circumstances in question, an unvirtuous belief will not be enough to justify this action, if it is justified from the internalist's standpoint. A virtuously held belief—one that is in my terms "subjectively justified"—will be required.

What now about the converse possibility? What about the possibility, in other words, of a virtuously held belief that fails to pass an internalist's standard of justification? How would this affect one's moral justification for acting on that belief?

Let us assume that such a case is possible. Say, owing to some slight logical flaw in one's reasoning, a given set of beliefs *B* does not justify belief *b*, even though one has virtuously reached the conclusion that *b* based on *B*. Would this impugn one's justification for acting? I would not think so, not unless one could fairly point to some *culpable* shortfall in one's examination of *B* and its implications. Failing such a shortfall, I would have to think that any failure of logical acumen is morally no different from, say, a failure of visual acuity. If I have done the best I can to determine whether the figure approaching is an enemy soldier and if I have determined that it is, I am, or certainly may be, justified in shooting. If I should be wrong owing to some failure of visual acuity, this would not have to count against the moral justification of my action. So, again, it seems clear that it is subjective justification in my sense, rather than justification in the internalist's sense, that relevantly determines moral justification.

Here it may be asked whether virtuously held belief is *always* required for justified action. In *emergencies* are we not justified in acting on beliefs that are not virtuously held? Let me state my view, then try to make it fairly plausible in terms of something like the previous example of identifying, and then firing at, an enemy soldier. In my view, when we must act on an excusably but not virtuously held belief, our action may plausibly be classed as, likewise, morally *excusable* but not justified.

First, suppose that there is a soldier on guard duty who happens to be subject to fits of extreme tension and who, having misidentified a friendly soldier as an enemy, precipitously shoots him. Here I want to say that insofar as we can excuse his forming that belief, perhaps, in view of his nervous condition, we can also excuse his action. But I would not call, nor does it seem intuitive to call, his action *justified*. It may be thought, however, that this case is somehow atypical, so let us alter the example slightly, removing the factor of the pathological condition. Suppose that the soldier simply misperceived the incoming individual, then immediately opened fire, killing his own man. His perception itself, we shall further suppose, was excusable, and he was entitled by his orders to "shoot immediately on identifying a hostile force." Now, one may look on such a case as involving a culpable failure to check or attend more closely to, the contents of one's perception before shooting, and in this case, the verdict must be that his action was culpable and unjustified. That, however, amounts to a claim that one's belief was subjectively *un*justified—if not upon its origination, at least at the slightly later point at which one acted on it.

Suppose, though, that we want to claim only that the perception was "automatic," neither reflecting any degree of virtue or culpable lack thereof. How does this affect the moral status of the consequent action? If the soldier's action were simply an immediate response to his misperception—so immediate as to preclude any judgment that "he ought to have made sure (or surer) before he shot"—then I would question whether the action truly deserves the label *justified*. Such a response would be, I would think, at *best* excusable. Recall our previous case (from section 1.2) of the soldier who is wired up in such a way as to fire merely on the formation of an appropriate belief. If this soldier excusably and spontaneously comes to believe that a figure in the distance is an enemy soldier, I would not want to call his subsequent firing justified so much as merely excusable. But perhaps it will be objected that his firing under these circumstances is not truly an *action* at all. If so, the example may be altered slightly so that he is wired in such a way that on formation of an appropriate intention or volition, he fires. If his firing is triggered under these circumstances, I am comfortable with the verdict of a merely excusable action.

Most emergencies, however, are not at all of this character. Most emergencies are such as to limit the extent of our reflective efforts but not such as to preclude some adequate, some appropriate degree of epistemic virtue. The actions and underlying beliefs of personnel in an emergency room are a perfect illustration of this. These are both legally and morally subject to considerable scrutiny. This is obviously no place for "negligence" of any sort, yet it is also hardly a place allowing for fine academic reflection and investigation. Rapid judgments must be made, judgments that are liable to be fallible. These judgments, however, are not made under circumstances which are so exigent as to preclude any possibility of virtuous efforts. By the same token, one's actions under these circumstances are plausibly counted as justified or unjustified according to the quality of one's underlying doxastic efforts. (Notice, even where an error were caused by some earlier omission—the intern was not aware of something he should have learned earlier on—this appeal to "doxastic efforts" is not out of place.)

4. Toward a Unified Normative Science: Ethics and Epistemology

The preceding discussion goes some distance toward establishing— what I find an intriguing goal—a unification of the two main normative disciplines of philosophy: ethics and epistemology. We have developed an account of (subjective) epistemic justification that ties in closely with the corresponding notion of moral justification and in three quite fundamental respects. First, our notion of epistemic justification is founded on notions of doxastic responsibility and voluntariness that closely mirror their moral counterparts. Second, the Humean reflections that provided a general rationale for this approach were themselves explicitly based on ethical, and only then applied to epistemic, matters. Third, our notion of epistemic justification itself is guided by the consideration that a justified belief ought to be one that one would be morally justified in acting on.

We have in general terms, then, explored the possibility of an approach to epistemic justification (and personal evaluation generally) in which the same formal concepts of virtue and responsibility are central, albeit with differences of content and differing notions of voluntariness (weak versus strong). However, can we go beyond these theoretical or overarching parallels and explore similarities of *content*, perhaps even similarities out of which we can understand the respective differences between these subjects as growing. To put the issue more provocatively, can we perhaps even discover respects in which the ethical and the epistemic are two branches growing out of a common source, a kind of undifferentiated "ur-concern?" Are there similarities of content uniting the moral and the epistemic virtues, as we have conceived the latter?

First, consider the virtue of *honesty*. Now, admittedly we think of honesty as a moral rather than as an epistemic virtue. But recall our earlier catalogue of the epistemic virtues in which the virtues of intellectual honesty form one of the three basic divisions of these. What the virtues of intellectual honesty share with the moral virtue of honesty is clearly one fundamental thing: a regard for the truth as such. Such regard becomes a distinctly moral virtue insofar as it involves contexts of communication with others. But, taken purely in itself, it does not seem, for example, that the unwillingness adequately to face or pursue the truth is, to the exclusion of the other, a moral or an epistemic failure. It is a *personal* failing that may certainly be seen as epistemic, but can be seen as moral as well.

The second personal virtue has no single, readily available name, but we may term it simply the "regard for others." Again, this is most readily understood as a moral virtue in a generic way, arguably as *the* moral virtue. But, recall too, that this is related to our second broad class of epistemic virtues: those of intellectual *impartiality*. These virtues we described as necessary to sustain an intellectual community; what they involve, most importantly, is a respect for others as possible sources of truth. This respect, one must also remember, involves an attitudinal or dispositional element that transcends that of a merely subjective "regard for others' ideas insofar as one thinks that they are likely to be true" and must include something less tied to one's own opinions at any given time. That is, it must include something like an genuine *openness* to others' ideas, which is not conditioned purely and simply by one's own opinions. And it is especially in this latter regard, I think, that we reach a normative level which is, at once and equally, ethical and epistemic. For even though such an openness to others' *ideas* does not constitute and cannot by itself generate the whole of our moral responsibilities to others, it certainly qualifies as a moral as much as an epistemic virtue. It certainly qualifies as a legitimate *part* of the total scope of our responsibilities to others. How, after all, are we to respect others as rational beings—a common theme of much of moral philosophy—if we lack due respect for their ideas, the distinctive product of their rationality?[4]

Probing a bit further, it is interesting to compare these two "ur levels" at which, as it were, morality meets epistemology. The first of these, honesty, clearly tends in the direction of the epistemic rather than the ethical. It is, one could say, an epistemic virtue that becomes ethical when an appropriate context is supplied (i.e., when we supply another person who stands to be misled by one's lack of honesty) or even when we think of intellectual dishonesty as an offense committed against oneself. The second of these, the regard for others, as though to balance the first, might appropriately be termed a moral virtue that becomes epistemic not so much by supplying a wider context as by narrowing its scope to certain aspects of others. Thus, it may be said that, on a somewhat further analysis, even our "ur virtues" are not entirely undifferentiated; they do carry a tag as more ethical than epistemic, or the reverse. To that extent at least, the distinction between belief and action—or, better, between morality and epistemology—is ultimate and irreducible.

Notes

1. See in this regard the *Treatise of Human Nature* (L.A. Selby-Bigge edition), pp. 411, 477, and 575.

2. It is important to understand in this connection that internalist concepts of justification may qualify as objective and not subjective in this sense. The internalist will restrict the range of "justifiers" of a given proposition to other propositions that the subject has access, but this by no means rules out a purely objective evaluation of the justificatory relationship holding among these. Of course, it is possible for an internalist view entirely to coincide with my own (with any such view I could hardly have any disagreements!); my point is merely that internalism need not take on this form.

3. One more recent criticism or implied criticism of subjective epistemic justification merits discussion in this connection. Kvanvig (cf. 1992, p. 67) would apparently maintain that a subjective characterization of justification is untenable because it would have to be understood—as Kent Bach (1985) and Kornblith (1983, 85) would wish to understand it—in terms of a subject's *acting* in a sufficiently exemplary way, thus, exempt-

ing from possible justification all beliefs that are not the result of any action. Two comments on this.

First, for reasons I have argued at some length in chapters 1 and 3, such a notion needn't be understood in terms of action but may and indeed must be understood in terms of a more basic power to exhibit conscientiousness and other epistemic virtues. Thus, to use Kvanvig's own example of Descartes' believing that he exists, this would qualify as justified, for Descartes, insofar as it passed reflective test. Whereas Kvanvig is surely right that this test would not involve an "action," he is not right if he wishes to suppose it did not require putting oneself into an appropriately attentive (epistemically conscientious) frame of mind, thereby to examine whether this was something clearly and distinctly perceived to be true.

The second comment, however, is that, as I have already conceded, on this view spontaneous perceptual beliefs will not count as justified. Now, Kvanvig wishes to insist that these *are* justified; but I think I am in at least as strong a position as he is on this point. I can and will gladly concede that these are justified in one important sense; I simply insist that in another sense they are not. Kvanvig, however, must maintain that in no important sense can such beliefs be spoken of as not justified. Prima facie, there is a sense of "justified" (what I call "subjectively justified") in which these beliefs are not. Because I think that Kvanvig's appeal to the concept of action (see my first comment) fails to undermine this sense of justified, for all he has so far shown, I think that we may feel relatively secure with this notion.

4.   To this it may be objected that openness to others' ideas is a virtue only insofar as these ideas are *rational*. My reply is this (cf. the discussion of the virtue of openness at section 2.2). We could shape this virtue as an openness to certain ideas insofar as they (on reflection) *seem* rational to one; but this runs the risk of being unduly subjective. Likewise, we could shape this virtue as an openness to certain ideas insofar as they actually are rational. But this, for reasons I indicate at section 2.3, becomes no longer a characterization of openness. It becomes something more like wisdom or one's being a "knowing" person. An openness to others, then, is a *tendency* that unchecked by other virtues (conscientiousness, intellectual courage), may degenerate into mere gullibility, which may *sometimes* lead one to embrace the irrational. But the same is true of the opposite virtue of intellectual courage.

Appendix One

Descartes and Doxastic Freedom

The argument of this appendix, which is an exposition and defense of the Cartesian theory of belief, is meant to accompany, strengthen, and provide a kind of historical background for the main, ongoing argument of the present study. As no part of it is absolutely essential to that argument, I have placed in at the end. But in one important respect it is more than a mere historical discussion. With Descartes, we have an example of a well-developed philosophical system in which one can, with suitable efforts, find the main claims of this study embedded. For instance, one finds a conception of the will and its relation to one's purely intellectual powers—to be sure, a much maligned conception whose employment requires defense, but still a conception I can use to fill out my own rather abstracted and asystematic approach to these questions. For as we shall see in this appendix, it is a conception ultimately wedded to a notion of direct doxastic control and responsibility.

1. Preliminary Reflections

I begin with some preliminary reflections concerning the relation between Descartes' account of belief in Meditation IV and the concerns motivating the present study. Descartes' overarching concern in this Meditation appears to be theological: how to reconcile human error with the perfection of our Creator. But what, I think, should most interest the contemporary, epistemologically minded reader of Meditation IV and what is relevant to our own discussion here is not this theological question, but instead the normative point on which Descartes' attempted theodicy rests: namely, that there are certain errors (certain false and unjustified beliefs) for which we are *to blame*—with respect to which we are "at fault." Intuitively, these will be cases in which our mistakes reflect not simply the limitations (or finiteness) of our powers of cognition, but, as Descartes is apt to say, their "misuse." As he also says at one point:

> [E]rror is not pure negation [i.e., is not the simple defect or want of some perfection which ought not to be mine], but it is a lack of some knowledge which it seems that I ought to possess. (HR I, p. 173)

I want to suggest, then, that we can understand Descartes' main question in Meditation IV as this. On what basis can we be truly faulted—genuinely *blamed*—for what we believe? Now in broad terms his answer to this question is clear enough. Where error is truly criticizable, and not only a reflection of the limits of our (finite) natures, it is due to the misuse of our doxastic freedom—to a misuse of that freedom, possessed by the will, which allows it not only to withhold assent from that which is unworthy of assent, but also to give assent to that which only seems to be so worthy. We are, more specifically, responsible for those errors of belief that result from a certain activity of will, whereby it affirms as true that for which our evidence is less than fully certain. Where we do *not* err, then, this is because we correctly make use of our will: by affirming that which is certain or by refusing to affirm that which is not.

2. The "Non-Neutral" Will

But what kind of will, or what kind of a view of the will, is thus presupposed by these contentions regarding doxastic freedom? Let us begin with some basic reflections. To the extent that that intentional action (under favorable circumstances) forms a kind of paradigm of that which is directly subject to one's control, the defender of doxastic freedom will be led to draw a deep analogy between the cases of action and belief. This analogy in a number of ways is suggestive both of Plato's and Kant's general philosophical conceptions, but its main idea is easily stated without reference to either of their views. It goes something like this. To a great extent we are creatures, both in our thoughts and actions, of spontaneous inclinations—inclinations to do this or that, inclinations to accept this or that as true. Often it turns out that we are guided by these inclinations—or by them plus such "instrumental" thinking we may use to figure out how best to attain the ends to which they prompt us. But, according to this idea, we are genuinely free—we are *masters* of these inclinations—to the extent that, guided by, as Descartes calls them (HR I, p. 175), "reasons of the good and the true," we are able to place limits on and countervail the power of these inclinations. Such is the essential activity of the will.

Notice, then, the will is not, on this conception, what might be termed simply a "neutral power of choice." That is, it is not conceived as equally free and able to direct itself at the good and the bad, the well and the ill conceived. Rather, it is, so to speak, intrinsically directed at the former member of each pair; and restrictions on its free operation, therefore, are seen specifically as restrictions on its opting for these.[1] So notice, too—although we shall come back to this subject at greater length in section A.5—it will not be true that on this view one's freedom consists somehow in believing (or doing) "whatever one would like." If I have no *reason* to do *x* or to believe *y*, then the fact that I may be unable to direct my will towards doing the one or believing the other is not, as such, an indication of a lack of freedom. To that extent, I may not be "free" to believe that the moon is made of green cheese, without this counting as a genuine restriction on my freedom of will. (In the terminology of chapter 5, this view, then, will not have to be committed to strong doxastic voluntarism.)[2]

In fact, the initial difficulty facing such a view as this is not in explaining how the will can freely direct itself at what it has every reason for thinking good or every reason for thinking true. Rather, as Sidgwick complained in the case of Kant,[3] this view gets into trouble in trying to explain how we can ever freely will what is wrong (or, in the doxastic case, freely assent to what one should not believe). We shall get to this difficulty momentarily, but first we may briefly admire Descartes' treatment of the case in which it does *not* arise: the case in which *p* is clearly and distinctly perceived. According to Descartes, not only are we free to believe what is clearly and distinctly perceived, when I embrace such a truth (or choose what is morally good) my freedom is at its height: The more clearly I recognize that "the reasons of the true" are to be found in adherence to *p*, "the more freely do I choose and embrace it" (HR I, p. 175). In this respect, one is free in much the way that a person, possessed of a clear view of and determination to take, the right course of action would experience the sudden onset of a contrary temptation only as an *impediment* to a free realization of his or her purposes—as making one less free, not more, despite the greater number of motivational possibilities that now are present. In short, on this Cartesian conception, one is free to the extent that certain intrinsically favored sources of action (or belief) are unimpeded by contrary inclinations or influences.

But as we turn to the case in which error *is* possible, an inevitable complication arises. Error takes place, in Descartes' memorable formulation, when the will is led to embrace "that which it does not understand" (i.e. something whose representation by the "understanding" is less than entirely clear and, thus falls "into error and sin" [HR I, 175–76]). Now, the complication is not that the will, when error occurs, has failed to find its appropriate end; for there is nothing in this non-neutral conception of the will that supposes that it could not sometimes be *overpowered* by a stronger force (inclination). Rather, the difficulty is that the will is now seen as *itself* embracing "error and sin." And how can the will do this if it is inherently oriented to seek the correct ends and is not a mere neutral mechanism of choice, sometimes identifying with the right and sometimes with the wrong?

The correct Cartesian response to this difficulty is, I think, suggested in the following passage, well-known, but not often cited in this connection. Of cases in which we embrace what is not clearly and distinctly perceived, Descartes writes:

> however probable are the conjectures which render me disposed to form a judgment respecting anything, the simple knowledge that I have that those are conjectures alone and not certain and indubitable truths, suffices to occasion me to judge the contrary. (HR I, 176)

Notice what Descartes says, and does not say, in this passage. He does not say that once I *do* understand *p* as merely "conjectural," that I am equally free to accept or reject it. Rather, his point might be better put in this way: Once I do understand *p* as conjectural, this recognition (in the absence of other influences or potential distractions) will *lead* me to reject *p*. Nor does Descartes say that before I recognize this merely probable status, I am free to reject *p*. If I were free to reject *p* even without this recognition of its doubtful status, it is puzzling why Descartes would lay such stress on the importance of *recognizing* that *p* is merely probable. (It is also puzzling how anyone could claim that I am free simply to reject what I had believed without coming to see its evidence as flawed in any way.) Return now to the difficulty concerning why the will should be attracted to error. The answer to this is that (on Descartes' view) the will is *not* attracted to error (or, presumably, to sin either)—at least, not as such. Recall that, on the above analysis, what attracted the will to assent to *p before* the recognition that it was merely probable was *p*'s seeming truth; and what repels the will after this recognition is *p*'s possible untruth. The point, then, could be put in this way: The will can be attracted by merely apparent truth, but it is never drawn to falsehood (or sin) as such.

This last point, however, gives rise to a new and potentially more serious concern. If the will is *simply* attracted to apparent truth and apparent good, it becomes pertinent to ask, what *good* is it? Obviously, and as noted earlier, we are *spontaneously* attracted to these (to apparent good and apparent truth); hence, if the will is to have any significant autonomy, or if it is to play anything like the *critical* role Descartes' envisions for it, obviously it must do more than follow spontaneous inclination. How, though, does it do this?

Let me close this first part of our discussion by indicating what is *not* a very satisfactory answer to the above question, even though it is suggested by Descartes' own presentation of the role of the will in formulating beliefs. On this familiar presentation, alluded to earlier, the special role of the will is apparently to assent or refuse assent to ideational contents provided by a distinct faculty— the understanding. Such a characterization of the powers of the will, however, only augments, or does little to mollify, the above concern that the Cartesian will might be but a "rubber stamp" for what is apparently good or true. For if the will itself is thus "blind" (to use Anthony O'Hear's suggestive term[4])—registering its approval based on nothing more than the ideas which the understanding gives it—how is the will supposed to play a critical role, or to exert its autonomy with respect to the cognitive realm?

3. Will and Understanding

We shall try to address these last concerns soon enough. But I will begin here by considering what the orthodox doxastic *involuntarist* is liable to say in response to the previous discussion.[5] I put the discussion as a dialogue.

Critic: Let us go back to your discussion of how one is supposedly "free" to reject what is merely conjectural. The basic problem I have is that your discussion fails to establish that one has any significant freedom, at any *given* point, either to embrace *p* or not to embrace *p*. Before I saw the limitations of *p*'s evidence (before

I saw *p* as merely probable), it does not seem that I was free to reject *p*; and *after* I saw *p* as merely so, it does not seem that I was free to accept *p* (with full conviction) any longer. At *no* point, then, does it seem that I am truly free *either* to embrace or reject *p*.

Descartes: Why should freedom require the existence of such "options?" You beg the question in favor of what I regard as a lower degree of freedom, the mere "liberty of indifference."

Critic: But if I have no effective option, when I do not *yet* perceive *p* to be merely conjectural, other than to accept *p*, then you must agree that I am not to *blame* for remaining in error. This potentially threatens your entire theory.

Descartes: Ah, you are right to this extent. If one were *only* free in this case to reject *p* once one saw that *p* was doubtful, it is true that this would not be enough. For there is the question of how one discovers, or might be free to discover, that *p* is doubtful in the first place.

Critic: How indeed? I'm always suspicious when I think a problem is being pushed back one step.

Descartes: Suppose, first, that I have already admitted as true something that in fact was really doubtful. You admit, of course, that it is possible for me to cease persisting in this error—possible for me to discover my error. But how do you think I am able to do this?

Critic: Perhaps you decide to rethink the issue; perhaps some new evidence is brought to your attention; perhaps you recall some old evidence which you had forgotten. There are any number of possibilities.

Descartes: Take the first of these. My question now is this. Why should it ever occur to you to reexamine the evidence?

Critic: I don't know. Maybe it occurs to me that I was not as careful as I should have been.

Descartes: Well, now we're getting somewhere. For my basic point is this. Absent new evidence (or old evidence suddenly recollected), it is only a determination of *will* whereby we decide, freely decide, to see whether *p* *really* must be true, given the evidence. Or I could put my point in this way. When I decide to look more closely, it is not the evidence that dictates this. By hypothesis, no new evidence has come in. So it is not the "understanding"—as I call it—it is the will, that dictates this. And this is a crucial respect in which we are free not only as agents, but as believers.

Critic: Go back one step, to this notion of "will" and "understanding." Correctly, you pointed out that we are able to reassess the evidence for *p* without the introduction of new evidence, or, in general, new reasons why we should do so. But what does this prove? I don't find the dichotomy of will and understanding very helpful—here or elsewhere. What it shows is that sometimes we are responsive not to particular evidentiary items, but instead to more *general* reflections concerning one's liability to make mistakes.

Descartes: You have succeeded in discovering what I would have maintained from the start: namely, that the activity of the will is governed by reasons; it is not a blind, incomprehensible "upsurge." Yes, the will is guided—and not only by an awareness of our liability for error, but by an *aversion* to such error and a corresponding love of the truth.

Critic: All right, I stand corrected on a relatively minor point. My larger question, though, goes unanswered. How is it that appeal to such general considerations succeeds in establishing a degree, or kind, of freedom that mere appeal to particular matters of evidence does not?

Descartes: All right here is my answer. With respect to what I call the understanding, we are fundamentally passive. The evidence strikes us in a certain way and we are thereby drawn to follow the direction of that evidence. This cannot be helped, because it is part of what it is to perceive something *as* evidence. It is clear, though, that we are not *entirely* passive in this connection, for we are able to withhold assent—again, without being prompted to do so (i.e., in a passive way) by new evidence.

Critic: But isn't the role of these general considerations (pertaining to the liability for error) by way of prompting the withholding of assent?

Descartes: You see, that is where you go astray. For what you fail to distinguish is a kind of passive role for such considerations— whereby they affect us when they happen to come to mind—and a truly active role for them—whereby we are able, on the basis of such considerations, actively to monitor the course of our doxastic lives.

Critic: I see the difference, but are you suggesting that we are always able to withhold assent? If so, I disagree.

Descartes: No I am aware and have written in the First Meditation of the persistence of our old, bad habits of belief. And I do not suppose, nor need I suppose, that we are constantly able to monitor these. It suffices to make my case that we are sometimes active in this regard without the promptings of the understanding. For if I am to blame for believing that *p*, it suffices that on *some* occasion—and, of course, this would not have to be upon acquisition of this belief—an effort of will would have enable me to recognize that the evidence for *p* was really weak.

Breaking off the dialogue here—with Descartes, I think, having more than held his own—let me try to underline and develop a bit further what I regard as its crucial point. Clearly we do recognize a difference between those occasions, rare as they may be, in which we are actively in control of our doxastic lives and those occasions, common as they may be, when we are merely responding to impulses (impulses that we consciously perceive as the promptings of *evidence* but that may unconsciously be the promptings of considerations related to what we desire, rather than to what we spontaneously think true). We don't, however, want to say—certainly Descartes will not want to say—that we are *capable* of such active responses only when in fact we offer them. For surely we want to leave open the possibility of what may often happen: namely, that we fail to be active when we *could* be so. Now, whether this "could" should be understood in a compatibilist way as hiding an "if" or whether it marks a point of absolute, "contracausal" freedom is not, I think, ultimately the crucial issue (cf. the discussion of this at section 3.5). The crucial issue is that we recognize this difference between the active expression of our autonomy and the merely passive response to the evidence with which we are constantly bombarded.

Finally, it may be wondered whether, by this point, we have not rejected Descartes' straightforward dichotomy of will as the faculty that passes judgment and understanding as the faculty that yields "ideas." Only to this extent. The will remains, on this view, the ultimate faculty of assent (and the withholding of assent). If, though, the "understanding" is to play a fully complementary role with respect to the will, it must be seen not merely in terms of generating ideas, but of *prompting* assent to these. It is, then, with respect to such prompts—or, perhaps better, with respect to our spontaneous inclinations to assent—that the will must assert its freedom. To revert now to O'Hear's metaphor (1972, p. 8), on this view, the will cannot fairly be described as "blind." The will oversees the spontaneous promptings of the understanding not blindly, but guided by its distinctively truth-oriented motivation and such general ideas as that one is apt to spontaneously assent to merely apparent truth. To this extent, the will is better seen as "the watchdog of the understanding" rather than the understanding as "the seeing-eye dog of the will."[6]

Let us now turn to something else, to some of the difficulties which Margaret Wilson (1978) has raised concerning Descartes' treatment of these matters, as we are now in a position to respond to these also.

As she moves from exposition to criticism of Descartes, Wilson writes that "according to the story of the Fourth Meditation, affirming obscure ideas is a lot like picking and eating apples in the dark. If in our greed for apples, or simple insouciance, we consume them all under palpably bad conditions of discrimination, we can't fairly blame God for our subsequent bellyaches." Summarizing this account, she says:

> I get myself into error just insofar as the following conditions hold:
> (a) I perceive my evidence for p is inadequate; (b) I decide to affirm
> p; (c) I forthwith, inwardly, commence to believe p. (p. 145).

This Wilson derides as a "very poor account." And in this she is, I think, correct; for, as she points out, if I perceive my evidence for *p* is inadequate, why should I decide to accept *p* especially if we do not consider, as Descartes apparently does not (cf. p. 144), such nonepistemic reasons as "wishful thinking?" Now, as Wilson points out, if we substitute something more like

(a)' I incorrectly perceive my evidence for *p* to be adequate,

it does become plausible why I should affirm *p* and thereby fall into error. Instead of postulating "arbitrary acts of will," Wilson suggests (p. 148), what Descartes should have said is that one can avoid error by coming to recognize in the case of (a)' that one's evidence is inadequate and, hopefully, giving up one's allegiance to *p*. Thus, on Wilson's reconstructed account, our doxastic freedom is, in Descartes' terms, transferred from the will to the understanding. That is, it will consist in our capacity to recognize (when I do not clearly and distinctly perceive that *p*) that I do not so perceive *p*.

Here, however, at least two criticisms of Wilson are in order. First, recalling the important passage quoted earlier concerning one's capacity to refrain from assent to mere conjectures, it seems fairly clear that Descartes intended something much more along the lines of (a)' than (a). For notice that what, on Descartes' account, the perception that the evidence for p is inadequate ("conjectural") occasions is not assent to p, but instead p's *rejection*. Thus, Descartes' actual view seems closer to Wilson's than she seems to realize; for, even on his view, it is the misperception of adequacy rather than the correct perception of inadequacy that leads to erroneous assent. Second, as the previous dialogue sought to bring out, barring the introduction of new evidentiary factors—what is required for me to *recognize* that the evidence for p is not compelling is the very Cartesian will that Wilson would have us dispense with. It is not the apparent state of the evidence, but instead a concern of the will (for truth) that directs me to look more closely, thus, enabling me to see flaws that I would not otherwise see.

4. Belief and the Will

What may look at this point like a more promising strategy against Descartes is this. Suppose that one concedes (however grudgingly) Descartes' position on the independence of the will relative to the understanding in order to focus critical pressure, instead, on the relation between the will and belief *itself*. Thus, it could be objected:

> The kind of control established by Descartes' argument goes this far and only this far. We are free to *try* to give or restrain assent. That is, we are free to direct ourselves to the effect that we ought or ought not to believe a given item. But, again recalling Descartes' own position in Meditation I, this is not to say that we are free to believe or not believe outright. For this is not to say that what we believe must always *conform* to such directives.

Something like this objection, too, is offered by Gassendi when he observes that, however much Descartes may seek to convince himself that he ought to refrain from judging that external objects exist (and so forth), he "cannot really have felt persuaded" that these propositions are not true whatever his protestations and resolutions to the contrary (cf. HR II, p. 181). For her part, Wilson makes almost exactly this same point in the following passage. Having observed that, on her reconstructed account of Descartes' theory, we are able to avoid falling into error by coming to recognize that we do not clearly and distinctly perceive p (when we do not), she wonders:

Is it always within our power to avoid forming an opinion when we perceive that the evidence for or against the proposition in question is less than adequate? It seems to me the answer is as follows: it is *empirically* implausible to suppose that our belief-formation is within our power to this extent. (p. 149)

But is this so "empirically implausible?" At issue, notice, is the relation between

(i) recognizing that my evidence for *p* is not fully adequate; (and)

(ii) coming no longer to believe that *p*.

One wonders, I think, whether this relation is actually as *remote* as Wilson apparently takes it to be? One imagines, in fact, Descartes as saying something like this:

In recognizing that my evidence is not fully adequate, I will direct myself not to believe this. If you prefer, I will judge that I "ought not to believe it." Now, whether or not this directive, or this ought-judgment, will be effective is, admittedly, quite another matter. I readily concede that it is quite possible not to believe what one directs oneself to believe. For instance, it is possible for a person to retain a belief based on old habits, unexamined prejudices, or simply a premature desire to settle the question in favor of one hypothesis rather than another,[7] even as she continues to acquire what has become a preponderance of evidence against this belief. The only problem I have with your description is that this person, you say, has *recognized* that the evidence stands against her belief. Would she not, by her very recognition of that, be rejecting her old belief—at least at that moment? I realize, of course, that old beliefs have ways of creeping back in. (cf. HR I, p. 148)

Still, a critic may find it odd that such a doxastic voluntarist as Descartes might have difficulty with the notion of believing one thing and recognizing the opposing state of the evidence. After all (the critic may allege), if the will is intrinsically sensitive not only to considerations of truth but moral concerns as well ("ideas of the good," as Descartes calls them), why should it not be possible for the will to be directed at what is morally best to accept as true rather than what the evidence supports?[8]

Let me answer for Descartes in this way. Obviously we do tend to believe for all sorts of cognitively bad reasons, including some morally good ones (even if this is rare). But I would not call such determination an expression of our doxastic *freedom*, for it marks a kind of absence of freedom: an inability of the will to pursue what are perceived as valid reasons for belief. Let me explain my thought here, by developing a distinction we have introduced already (cf. section 3.2). There is a logical and psychological difference between recognizing that q is a reason to think p *true* and q is a reason why it would be good (or moral) for one to *believe* that p. It is this. In recognizing that q (which I already believe) is a reason to believe p, I am *thereby* putting some credence in p.[9] The two, in other words, are not wholly separate thoughts. For what is it to put credence in something if it is not to recognize the existence of a reason, or reasons, for thinking it true? By contrast, in recognizing that q (which again I already believe) is a reason why it would be good (or moral) if I believed p, I am not thereby led to put credence in p. Rather, I am led to put credence in a different proposition: one to the effect that it would be good if I were to *bring it about* that I believe p. Notice, then, if this is correct, the basic autonomy (independence) of the realms of theoretical and practical reason is preserved. Reasons for thinking true have the same immediate relation to belief that reasons for thinking something good have to *action*. The case where this "something thought good" is the having of a *belief*, then, should not mislead. Such thoughts may influence belief, but only by way of their more direct bearing on action. Genuine reasons for belief (thinking *true*) know no such limitation.

Finally, going back a bit, let me comment on the connection between (i) and (ii) above, which was the original point of contention. By extending the previous argument one can see that this connection must be extremely close, close enough to defeat any suggestion that the relation between them might be empirically remote. For if recognizing that q is a reason to believe p true counts as putting some (perhaps minimal) credence in p, recognizing that q is a *sufficient* reason to believe p true must count as putting considerable credence in p. Clearly, in default of special, countervailing factors, recognizing the sufficiency of evidence for p will be one way of affirming p.[10]

5. Unrestricted Voluntarism

It is instructive to compare the view taken here of the Cartesian will and its powers to two rather different views. The first, to be considered in this section, ascribes essentially an *unlimited* doxastic freedom: a freedom to believe whatsoever one wishes, with the possible exception of willing the denial of what is clearly and distinctly perceived. (The second, to be considered in the next section, attributes a *lesser* freedom to the will [i.e., an ability to control belief only via controlling action].)

Let us consider what may be cited on behalf of and against the more expansive interpretation of Descartes.[11]

First, there is the passage in Meditation IV, which we now consider in a different connection, in which Descartes seems to assert a stronger power than one of merely refraining from belief under conditions of uncertainty. Speaking of propositions that he recognizes to be merely "conjectures," he allows not only that we can withhold assent from these, but that we can actually succeed in judging "the contrary," (i.e., in getting ourselves to "set aside as false" this proposition [HR I, p. 176]). In this same connection, Descartes refers to his earlier resolution (of Meditation I) that he will not simply suspend judgment with respect to his former opinions, but actually "pretend" that they are "entirely false and imaginary" until such time as these cease to dominate his thought and judgment (HR I, p. 148). Now, is not Descartes suggesting here a much stronger view according to which we can and should not merely abstain from assent to the probable, but actually embrace the *im*probable (even if temporarily)? Is Descartes not suggesting that he will not only abstain from judging that "I have seen the sun," but actually judge that it is false that I have seen the sun, therefore, true that I have *not* seen the sun? And if I can judge that I have not seen the sun, can I not judge (believe) pretty much whatsoever I will?

Let me here explain why I think that Descartes should not be read as intending to go that far.

First, any such belief would contradict the guiding maxim of his entire philosophy: only to believe what is clearly and distinctly perceived to be true. In all of the cases in question, neither *p* nor the denial of *p* is clearly and distinctly perceived to be true; hence, under these conditions, Descartes can hardly be recommending that one form a settled conviction that *p* is false any more than that *p* is true. (Of course, he does not clearly and distinctly perceive that he has not seen the sun.) Second, in the passage quoted from Meditation I, Descartes is speaking from the standpoint of one who believes that, under the conditions described, one should really abstain from believing either *p or* its negation. That is the goal of his little stratagem: He will, he says, try to get himself to reject *p* as false by a kind of self-deception; but he does not now believe that *p* is false, nor does he wish ultimately to hold that belief.

There is another passage, which certainly deserves consideration here, where Descartes apparently asserts an even stronger doctrine of doxastic control. This is in his well-known letter (apparently) to Mesland[12] in which, in the course of a general discussion of freedom of the will, Descartes goes so far as to say that

> it is always open to us to hold back from pursuing a clearly known good, or from admitting a clearly perceived truth, provided we consider it a good thing to demonstrate the freedom of our will in so doing. (p. 27)

Now, surely, if we can reject as false what seems most evident to us, we truly could believe anything we like. But does Descartes really say that we can reject "as false" that which is clearly perceived to be true? Anthony Kenny (1972, p. 29) has suggested that what Descartes meant was only that, insofar as we are not at a given point clearly perceiving *p* to be true (or recognizing the grounds there are for regarding *p* as certain), that we may reject *p*—again, if only to demonstrate the freedom of the will. This reading has the virtue of squaring Descartes' contention here with the many places in which he says that we cannot doubt what is clearly and distinctly perceived. Nonetheless, I find Kenny's reading implausible. For it is just not plausible that such truths as 1 = 1 can be denied, regardless of whether one is thinking of the grounds one might have for them. (Try denying that 1 = 1 to demonstrate freedom of the will.) To this Kenny may reply that we cannot help thinking of the grounds of such truths, but then his interpretation fails to square with Descartes' apparent insistence that we can *always* deny that which we clearly perceive. Instead, what Descartes seems to mean here, I think, is just this. Even if I perceive *p* to be evident, I can refrain from the *action* of "admitting it to be true" even if not from the belief itself. This, I would suppose, is why Descartes distinguishes in the sentences preceding the quoted passage one's "moral" inability to make such a denial from one's "absolute" ability to do so. Morally, I am bound to admit as true what

I clearly and distinctly perceive to be so, just as morally I am bound to pursue what I clearly see to be good. But absolutely I am not bound to pursue the latter or to admit the former—which, again, is not to say that I am able to *believe* that what I clearly and distinctly perceive is false.

Finally, deserving of some mention in this connection are such statements of Descartes' as that the will "may in some measure be said to be infinite" (HR I, p. 233); or that we recognize it to be "so extended as to be subject to no limits" (HR I, p. 174). Do these passages suggest that Descartes holds that one can believe at will any proposition one likes, or perhaps, as Peter Markie has suggested (1983, p. 103), any *true* proposition one likes? Not at all. First, if Descartes meant the "unlimited" character of the will to enable one to believe anything one liked, he would not have insisted that we are unable to believe (at will or otherwise) the negation of what we clearly and distinctly perceive. Let us turn, then, to Markie's problem. Markie suggests that, on Descartes' view, a person might believe at will a true proposition for which she lacked adequate evidence. But here Markie needs to make it clear whether the individual clearly recognizes this absence of adequate evidence. If she *clearly* sees that the evidence is inadequate, then she will not and cannot affirm this as true, and, by the previous argument, this will be entirely consistent with the "unlimited" character of the will. If, however, she does not clearly see this, then the case becomes the familiar one from section A.2: the case of affirming the doubtful when one does not perceive it as doubtful.

The main lesson of this section, then, quite agrees with the conclusion of its predecessor. Given the argument of the preceding section, we should not think it possible that we can believe whatever we would like (irrespective of questions of evidence), for that would require that belief in the same direct way on the basis of practical, as well as epistemically relevant, considerations. Here we have seen that there is no very convincing textual evidence that Descartes allows any such freedom, which is just what he should say, if I have been right.

6. Direct versus Indirect Cartesian Voluntarism

I have left for last what is, from the larger standpoint of this essay, perhaps the most important question of all. As far back as the first chapter of this study, we have noted that epistemic norms, even where they imply such notions of "culpability" for one's beliefs, do *not* have to be interpreted as requiring direct doxastic control, but may be thought to require only indirect control of one's beliefs (exerted via control over one's actions). To be sure, we argued in that first chapter that the latter view is unsuccessful. But does *Descartes'* program require a notion of direct, or only indirect, control? If we can show, as I do hope to show, that Descartes' program requires a direct notion, this can only strengthen confidence that I have been on the right track.

But let us begin by considering the case to be made on the other side, that Descartes need only be construed as an indirect voluntarist. We may think of the involuntarist case as starting from the notion that what Descartes is after is a form of *therapy* (cf. Marlies [1978]), a therapy that will over time change our underlying doxastic dispositions to the point that we successfully internalize a new criterion of acceptance: namely, to accept as true only what is clearly and distinctly perceived. Such a course will evidently require appropriate meditative efforts, subjecting oneself to the right environmental influences, but these are all appropriate actions. In this regard, it would not seem that Descartes' methods of achieving epistemic rectitude are as different in kind from Pascal's remedies for achieving faith. Both are indirect.

How do I reply to this case? Let us begin by considering the epistemically proper habits that the aforementioned therapeutic efforts are supposed to bring about. Query: Are these simply habits by which the person responds in an appropriate but automatic way to evidentiary inputs; or are these, at least in part, habits of maintaining a properly vigilant, careful, and concerned attitude?

Consider, then, the first of these possibilities. Notice, on this supposition, our entire doxastic responsibility will be pushed backed to the point at which these automatic tendencies were inscribed. For, on this supposition, the idea is that there is no active role for will, or what I would call virtuous efforts, in the actual exercise of these habits. Once in place, they work well (or ill)—without any further efforts. But now to confront this view with some basic questions. How is it that one is responsible for the creation (or perhaps the final maturation) of these habits, but not their exercise? May we fault a person by claiming that "you ought, at or before time t, have developed a better epistemic habit"? But why, then, did they not? Presumably, this was either because they did not recognize the desirability of doing so or because, while recognizing this, they were just insufficiently motivated to bring about this admittedly desirable state of affairs. Well, what of these? If one could be held responsible for failing to recognize this desirability, one has been held responsible—it would certainly seem—for not forming an appropriate *belief*. If, moreover, one can be held responsible for not recognizing this desirability, there seems little reason to reject the notion I defended at sections 4.2–4.4 of a *continuing* responsibility one has to recognize particular situations as calling for virtuous efforts. For each act of recognition would seem to be equally subject to one's control.

Consider, then, the second possibility. Suppose that I do recognize the desirability of setting up an appropriate habit but am simply unmotivated, or insufficiently motivated, to do the necessary work to bring this about. Now, "unmotivated" in this connection may be, I think, understood in either of two ways. Either this refers to the absence of—call it—the "energy" required to do this, or it refers in a somewhat more intellectual way to one's not seeing sufficient reason to do it. But the second of these merely recapitulates the possibility we have just considered (of not recognizing the desirability of setting up the habit in question). And the first of these can hardly be termed something for which one is responsible (at the time in question).

So I reject the supposition—what was exceedingly strange to begin with—that we are only responsible at the moment when such sound Cartesian habits were originally set up. We are left, then, with the alternative view that the exercise of these habits is accomplished, through some effort for which we are properly held responsible. But now we have backed our way into a view that is entirely compatible with the one defended in this study.[13]

One last point. It may be asked whether Descartes does not think that correct belief requires a correct *criterion* of what ought to be believed. And, assuming that he does, am I not saddling Descartes with the unpromising thesis that we can control, at will and at any given point, what criterion we have?[14]

To respond to this, we must first distinguish the Cartesian *ideal* from what, at any given point, is possible for a person—thus, what, at any given time, a person can be blamed for failing to attain. The attainment of Descartes' ideal certainly does require knowledge (and internalization) of a correct criterion. But the road to this criterion begins, and continues to depend on, something more basic, an attitudinal requirement of a conscientious regard for truth. At *some* point, hopefully, this attitude comes to express itself as an adherence to a correct criterion of knowledge; but clearly, it is the right attitude that must come first, and it is failures in regard to this attitude which are the subject of our ultimate doxastic responsibility.

Notes

1. This "asymmetrical" conception—wherein action that accords with one's values or better judgment is, one might say, inherently freer than action that runs against these—is a deep current in compatibilist views of free action: cf. Harry Frankfurt (1971), Gary Watson (1975), and Susan Wolf (1980).

2. So, if this is right, Descartes' version of doxastic voluntarism is not in any obvious way open to the main objection raised by such authors as Price (1954) and Alston (1988) against extreme formulations of doxastic voluntarism, namely that these views allow that we can believe, by a simple act of will, whatever we would like. On this point, see Williams (1978, pp. 178ff).

3. See the appendix ("The Kantian Conception of Free Will"), Sidgwick (1907).

4. (1972, p. 102). O'Hear, however, does not—at least to my satisfaction—succeed in explaining how and why the will is *not* blind on Descartes' account. (See below, in the text.)

5. The discussion that follows may be instructively compared to certain objections posed against Descartes by Gassendi (cf. HR II, p. 181) and, even more to the point, with Descartes' own reply to these (HR II, p. 225). I place special emphasis on Descartes' point that doxastic freedom is a presupposition of *"how we can refrain from persisting in error"* (Descartes' emphasis).

6. In denying that the will is "blind," I do *not* want to say, with Hiram Caton (1975, p. 102), that the will adds a special *content*, not perceived—or at least not provided—by the understanding, and thereby falls into error (when error occurs). If we ask whether the understanding perceives this new content, then a dilemma results. If it does, then why we need to associate its cause as the will is unclear. The function of the will is going remain that of assenting to what is in this case an unclear perception of the understanding. If, however, the understanding does not perceive this added content, then we are totally outside of Descartes' intended dichotomy.

7. Compare in this regard chapter 2, note 5. Of course, if we are to be *responsible* for the display of such vices, these must be things we permit either by culpably failing to exert a sufficient concern for truth at the time they occur (a distinctively Cartesian position) or by culpably at

some earlier time failing to do what was required not to have this habit develop, more the Aristotelian position.

8. This is the view of Meiland (1980). Meiland urges, what we have allowed, that a person can recognize the evidence for p to be "sufficient" without believing p (p. 17). He does *not*, however, argue that, or consider the question of whether, a person can believe on the basis of moral considerations in the same way in which she can believe on the basis of epistemic ones. On this, see below in the text.

9. It may be objected that putting "credence" in something may involve no more than thinking it true regardless of whether one regards it as having reasons or evidence to support it. This may well be correct; however, my claim here is really only the converse: that regarding p as supported by evidence (or good epistemic reasons for thinking true) is ipso facto putting credence in p.

10. Ironically, E. M. Curley (1975, p. 175) cites this close connection between (i) and (ii) as posing a *difficulty* for Descartes [since it would mean that one's control with respect to (ii) is limited at best, given that one instantiates (i)]. But this is only a problem if one thinks—what I would deny—that doxastic freedom would only be genuine if it were exerted at the level of (ii), on the basis of a previous judgment with respect to the evidence. I want to suppose that this freedom is most often exerted simply at the level of (i)—and (*pace* Curley) only *thereby* at the level of (ii).

11. Anthony Kenny (1968, p. 24) and Louis Pojman (1986, p. 145) are among those who understand Descartes as making the claim that we are able to believe at will anything which is not the negation of what we clearly and distinctly perceive.

12. See in this regard Anthony Kenny's (1972), which includes a translation and commentary on this important letter. The reference which follows is from this source.

13. Jeff Tlumak (1983) takes Descartes' voluntarism to be indirect in part because, as he correctly points out, Descartes thinks that we can only have the right sort of dispositions to believe through careful, prior training of the mind—and not by anything like an immediate act of will. Descartes does not think, says Tlumak, that "at any given time I can believe what I want or what I ought to believe; [o]therwise doubt therapy would be unnecessary" (p. 92). I would reply as follows. Believing what I want (cf. note 6 and the accompanying text) would not be required for voluntary control; moreover, since I am *compelled* to believe what I ought to believe (what I clearly and distinctly perceive), it is an oversight on Tlumak's part to deny one's immediate power to believe this. What, I think, Tlumak means to say is that often I am not able to *refrain* from believing what I ought not to believe. This, as we have seen, however,

covers basically two cases: one in which I do not recognize the insufficiency of my evidence (discussed in section A.3) and one in which I do (discussed in section A.4). In both cases, I have argued, Descartes' account requires a point at which we have direct, and not just indirect, control over what we accept as true.

14.   On this point, I think that I differ with both Tlumak (1983, p. 92) and O'Hear (1972, p. 108), both of whom wish to regard doxastic freedom as based on the freedom to select such a criterion of rational acceptance.

Appendix Two

Normative Epistemology

An important and currently lively topic in epistemology is the nature and source of whatever *norms* with which this subject is distinctively concerned. Is epistemology a "normative" subject? If so, with what norms is it concerned and how are these to be justified? What relation obtains between epistemology as a normative discipline and the familiar slogan of W.V.O. Quine (1969) of "epistemology naturalized?" These are among the related questions lurking here—and large ones they are. But we can be reasonably direct in our answers to them if—as is entirely appropriate at this stage in the proceedings—we stay basically within the confines of the view developed to this point.

First, it will be useful to distinguish two kinds, or levels, of normative epistemology. A "Level One" normative epistemology will offer, among other things, epistemic *prescriptions* of the form "*S* ought not to believe *p*" or "It was wrong of *S* to believe *p*" or "It was not good that *S* believed *p*." It will yield, in other words, value judgments grounded in epistemic, rather than moral or other practical considerations, concerning the beliefs of individuals. What a Level One epistemology will *not* be committed to, however, is to is the claims we have freely indulged concerning epistemic voluntariness, blameworthiness, and responsibility. It will not, that is, yield such propositions such as "*S* is culpable for believing *p*," "*S* should not have opted to believe *p*," "*S* is responsible for believing *p*"—and the like. Call, then, the embrace of such propositions a "Level Two" normative epistemology.

Obviously, ours has been, unabashedly, a Level Two epistemology. What may be less obvious is the source of epistemic norms on this view. From what considerations do such norms derive their *authority*? Why is it, exactly, that one ought to follow these norms?

A proper answer to this demands a short excursus, relating to the inevitably *external* character of the norms on any Level One epistemology. On such a view, since there is no particular requirement that an individual actually be able to follow a given norm, norms are simply requirements in *comparison* to which beliefs may be examined. In this regard, they are no different, say, from norms—based on the past performances of great thoroughbreds—to which the performances of horses today might be judged. Notice, this is true even in the case of the Level One internalist. Even though this internalist requires that justificational norms draw on materials that are internal to the believer—materials to which the believer has "access"—if the believer is unable to believe on the basis of these, any requirement that she do so is as much an external imposition as a requirement that a $10,000 yearling run like Secretariat.

The authority, then, of such norms will reflect this external character. It may derive from something like an *intuition* that truth ought to be pursued; it may derive from the subject's own *standing* desire to have true beliefs; it may derive from the advisability of having true beliefs no matter what one's other ends, as with Kornblith's (1991).[1] But it will not be internal in the sense of bearing—or, better, having to bear—some immediate relation to the agent's actual motives in forming a given belief.

I need to point out here, however, that internalism (in the sense we are using this term) is not to be equated simply with the view that "ought implies can" lest there be no defensible version of ethical externalism. Thomas Nagel makes the relevant point here nicely (1970, ch. 3) in distinguishing two different forms of ethical internalism. What both share (besides a notion that "ought implies can") is a notion that the characteristic motivation for following ethical requirements should *coincide* with the considerations in virtue of which one ought to act in these ways. (Morality, in short, should provide its own motivational backing and should not rely, willy-nilly, on the presence of nonmoral motives for meeting moral requirements.) Where these types of internalism differ is in this regard: the non-Kantian sort favored by such empirically minded philosophers as Hume and Hobbes bases ethical norms on independently discoverable features of human psychology (such as the fear of death, for Hobbes). The Kantian sort of internalism proceeds differently, by identifying certain ethical principles which are, as Nagel puts it,

> themselves propositions of motivation theory so fundamental that
> they cannot be derived from or defined in terms of previously

understood motivations. . . . Thus, they *define* motivational
possibilities, rather than presupposing them. (p. 14)

Such a motivational factor is Kant's notion of "respect" for the
moral law (cf. section 3.4); another is what I have termed "epistemic
conscientiousness." Like Kant's notion, it is not an independently
discoverable feature of human psychology on which we attempt to
base epistemic norms; rather it is a psychological motivation that
is discovered only in the context of observing the workings of
epistemic norms.

Are, then, epistemic norms to be viewed as somehow "categorical imperatives?" I am not entirely happy with this solution and
for this reason. Whereas the motivation to be conscientious is, in
one sense, internal to the process of arriving at and monitoring
beliefs, in another sense, it is not. That is, even though the belief
acquisition process necessarily involves some motivation to pursue
truth, recall that, in most instances, we are *prompted* to be conscientious only through the recognition of the special importance of
believing correctly (in that particular circumstance). (Compare in
this regard the discussion of sections 4.2–4.3.) Hence, reverting
again to Nagel's distinction, the motivation to be epistemically
conscientious *does* rest in part on independently discoverable motives (typically of morality or self-interest, but possibly ones of
longer-term epistemic consequences), and not on a motivational
factor which is purely internal to the belief process.

To this extent, the norms of epistemology—where they are
categorical—ride piggy-back on categorical nonepistemic (presumably, *moral*) norms. Even though being conscientious involves an
intrinsic motivation towards truth, the requirement that one exhibit
this motivation is not, at least not normally, based on purely epistemic considerations. My kind of normative epistemology, then, falls
short of the pure Kantian-Nagelian ideal of an entirely internal
system: The sources of whose validity and motivation are identical
and not derived from an external source.

Finally, there is the matter of "naturalized epistemology"—or of
its relation to normative epistemology as conceived here. I have
already conceded (section 6.2) that a virtue-based normative epistemology is essentially incomplete, conceded that it does not provide an account of the objective conditions under which a belief is
justified—recall, as opposed to the conditions under which a person is justified in believing something. Continuing now this line of
thought, I would want to say that investigation of such objective

conditions certainly would constitute a naturalized epistemology. But why, more fundamentally, do we need such an epistemology and what relation should it be expected to be to normative epistemology? Briefly, my answer is this. If normative epistemology is responsive to the first-person perspective and its distinctive limitations, which require that ultimately one can only act on one's *own* best assessment of the situation, such a naturalized epistemology is responsive to the third-person perspective and our distinctive interest in this. If I am told that Jones has a "justified" belief that *p*, assuming that I am interested in Jones's belief (as opposed to *Jones*), this interests me mainly insofar as the relevant notion of justification is *objective*, not subjective. Only the first of these gives me very good reason to *rely* on this belief of Jones. Jones may be enclosed within an egocentric predicament (and I am enclosed within an egocentric predicament of my own); but I am not enclosed in Jones's predicament and obviously would have little to gain by pretending to be so limited.

Normative epistemology—as I see it—is not a characterization of facts about the world which we need to know for anything other than philosophical (including ethical) purposes. It is fundamentally a description of the egocentric predicament and its logical consequences for epistemology and ethics. Non-normative (naturalized) epistemology, by contrast, is simply part and parcel of what we want to know about the world—in this case, to facilitate knowing even more about the world.

Note

1.   This paper contains a number of well-taken criticisms of the views of Goldman (1986), Stich (1990), and Quine (1990) on the basis of epistemic norms.

References

With the exception of classic works like *The Critique of Practical Reason*, texts are cited by author and date of original publication. Where I have used pagination from some reprinted version, this later version is also cited in this list. This, for the most part, is a list of actual citations, rather than a bibliography.

Adams, Robert. (1984). "The Virtue of Faith," *Faith and Philosophy* 1, reprinted in the collection of his essays, *The Virtue of Faith* (Oxford: Oxford University Press, 1987), 9–24.

Alston, William. (1985). "Concepts of Epistemic Justification," *The Monist* 68, reprinted in Alston's *Epistemic Justification* (Ithaca, NY: Cornell University Press, 1989), 81–114.

———. (1986). "Internalism and Externalism in Epistemology," *Philosophical Topics* 14, reprinted in *Epistemic Justification* (Ithaca, NY: Cornell University Press, 1989), 185–226.

———. (1988). The Deontological Conception of Epistemic Justification," in James Tomberlin, ed., *Philosophical Perspectives*, reprinted in *Epistemic Justification* (Ithaca, NY: Cornell University Press, 1989), 115–52.

Aquinas, Saint Thomas. (1963). *Summa Theologica*, Blackfriars editions, volume 23, W. D. Hughes, trans., (New York: McGraw-Hill).

Aristotle. (1941). *Nicomachean Ethics*, W. D. Ross, trans., in Richard McKeon, ed., *The Basic Works of Aristotle* (New York: Random House).

Audi, Robert. (1978). "Psychological Foundationalism," *The Monist*, 61, 592–610.

———. (1983). "The Causal Structure of Indirect Justification," *Journal of Philosophy* 80, 398–415.

———. (1991). "Responsible Action and Virtuous Character," *Ethics* 101, 304–21.

Bach, Kent. (1985). "A Rationale for Reliabilism, *The Monist*, 68, 246–63.

Bennett, Jonathan. (1990). "Why is Belief Involuntary?" *Analysis*, 50, 87–107.

Bernstein, Mark. (1986). "Moral and Epistemic Saints," *Metaphilosophy* 17, 102–8.

Bonjour, Laurence. (1980). "Externalist Theories of Empirical Knowledge," *Midwest Studies in Philosophy* 5, 53–73.

Bullock, Allan. (1962). *Hitler: A Study in Tyranny* (New York: Harper and Row).

Caton, Hiram. (1975). "Will and Reason in Descartes's Theory of Error," *Journal of Philosophy*, 72, 87–104.

Chisholm, Roderick. (1968). "C. I. Lewis's Ethics of Belief," in P. A. Schilpp, ed., *The Philosophy of C. I. Lewis* (LaSalle, IL: Open Court), 223–42.

———. (1991). "Firth and the Ethics of Belief," *Philosophy and Phenomenological Research*, 51, 117–28.

Clarke, Murray. (1986). "Doxastic Voluntariness and Forced Belief," *Philosophical Studies*, 50, 39–51.

Clifford, William K. (1877). "The Ethics of Belief," reprinted in Gerald D. McCarthy, ed., *The Ethics of Belief Debate* (Atlanta: Scholar's Press, 1986), 19–36.

Code, Lorraine. (1983). "Fathers and Sons: A Case Study in Epistemic Responsibility," *The Monist*, 66, 268–82.

Cohen, L. Jonathan. (1989). "Belief and Acceptance," *Mind*, 98, 365–89.

Conee, Earl. (1987). "Evident, But Rationally Unacceptable," *Australasian Journal of Philosophy*, 68, 321–26.

Conee, Earl and Richard Feldman. (1985). "Evidentialism," *Philosophical Studies*, 48, 15–34.

Cook, Thomas. (1987). "Deciding to Believe Without Self-Deception," *Journal of Philosophy*, 84, 441–46.

Curley, E. M. (1975). "Descartes, Spinoza and the Ethics of Belief," in M. Mandelbaum and E. Freeman, eds. *Spinoza: Essays in Interpretation* (LaSalle, IL: Open Court), 159–90.

Davidson, Donald. (1971). "Agency" in *Actions and Events* (Oxford: Oxford University Press, 1978), 43–61.

De Sousa, Ronald. (1971). "How To Give a Piece of Your Mind; or, The Logic of Belief and Assent," *Review of Metaphysics* 25, 52–79.

Descartes, Rene. (1970). *The Philosophical Works of Descartes*, two volumes, Elizabeth Haldane and G.R.T. Ross, trans. (Cambridge: Cambridge University Press).

Donagan, Alan. (1977). *The Theory of Morality* (Chicago: University of Chicago Press).

Evans, J. L. (1963). "Error and the Will," *Philosophy*, 38, 136–48.

Feldman, Richard. (1985). "Subjective and Objective Justification in Ethics and Epistemology," *The Monist*, 68, 407–19.

Firth, Roderick. (1981). "Epistemic Merit, Intrinsic and Instrumental," *Proceedings of the American Philosophical Association,* 55, 149–156.

Foley, Richard. (1987). *The Theory of Epistemic Rationality* (Cambridge, MA: Harvard University Press).

Frankfurt, Harry. (1971). "Freedom of the Will and the Concept of a Person," *Journal of Philosophy*, 68, 5–20.

Gale, Richard. (1980). "William James and the Ethics of Belief," *American Philosophical Quarterly*, 17, 1–14.

Gassendi, Pierre. (1970). "Letter from P. Gassendi to M. Descartes" (The Fifth Set of Objections to Descartes's Meditations) in *Philosophical Works of Descartes*, volume two (Cambridge: Cambridge University Press), 135–203.

Gilson, Etienne. (1947). *Discours de la Méthode: Texte et Commentaire* (Paris: Librairie Philosophique).

Ginet, Carl. (1975). *Knowledge, Perception and Memory* (Dordrecht: D. Reidel).

Goldman, Alvin. (1980). "The Internalist Conception of Justification," *Midwest Studies in Philosophy*, 5, 27–51.

———. (1986). *Epistemology and Cognition* (Cambridge, MA: Harvard University Press).

Harman, Gilbert. (1975). "Moral Relativism," *Philosophical Review*, 89, 3–22.

Heil, John. (1983a). "Doxastic Agency," *Philosophical Studies*, 46, 355–64.

———. (1983b). "Believing What One Ought," *Journal of Philosophy*, 80, 752–65.

———. (1984). "Doxastic Incontinence," *Mind*, 93, 56–70.

Hobart, R. E. (1934). "Free Will as Involving Determinism and Inconceivable Without It," *Mind*, 63, 1–27.

Hume, David (1967). *Treatise of Human Nature*, L. A. Selby-Bigge, ed. (Oxford: Clarendon Press, 1967).

Hunt, Lester H. (1978). "Character and Thought," *American Philosophical Quarterly*, 15, 177–86.

James, William. (1897). "The Will to Believe," in McCarthy, ed., *The Ethics of Belief Debate* (Atlanta: Scholar's Press, 1986), 55–72.

Kane, Robert. (1985). *Free Will and Values* (Stony Brook: State University of New York Press).

Kant, Immanuel. (1956). *Critique of Practical Reason*, Lewis Beck, trans. (Indianapolis: Bobbs-Merrill).

Kaplan, Mark. (1981). "Rational Acceptance," *Philosophical Studies*, 40, 129–45.

Kenny, Anthony. (1968). *Descartes: A Study of His Philosophy* (New York: Random House).

———. (1972). "Descartes on the Will," in R. J. Butler, ed., *Cartesian Studies* (New York: Barnes and Noble).

Kornblith, Hilary. (1983). "Justified Belief and Epistemically Responsible Action," *Philosophical Review*, 92, 33–48.

———. (1985). "Ever Since Descartes," *The Monist*, 68, 264–76.

————. (1991). "Epistemic Normativity" (typescript).

Kvanvig, Jonathan. (1986). "How to be a Reliabilist," *American Philosophical Quarterly*, 23, 189–97.

————. (1992). *The Intellectual Virtues and the Life of the Mind* (Lanham, MD: Rowman and Littlefield).

Lehrer, Keith. (1974). *Knowledge* (Oxford: Oxford University Press).

————. (1981). "Self-Profile," in Radu Bogdan, ed., *Keith Lehrer* (Dordrecht: D. Reidel), 3–104.

————. (1990). *Theory of Knowledge* (Boulder, CO: Westview Press).

Markie, Peter. (1983). "Descartes's Theory of Judgment," *Southern Journal of Philosophy*, 21, 101–10.

Marlies, Mike. (1978). "Doubt, Reason and Cartesian Therapy," in Michael Hooker, ed., *Descartes: Critical and Interpretive Essays* (Baltimore: Johns Hopkins University Press).

Meiland, Jack. (1980). "What Ought We to Believe? or The Ethics of Belief Revisited," *American Philosophical Quarterly*, 17, 15–24.

Mele, Alfred R. (1986). "Incontinent Believing," *The Philosophical Quarterly*, 36, 215–22.

Montmarquet, James. (1985). "Epistemological Internalism," *Southern Journal of Philosophy*, 23, 229–40.

————. (1986). "The Voluntariness of Belief," *Analysis*, 46, 49–53.

————. (1987a). "Epistemic Virtue," *Mind*, 96, 482–97.

————. (1987b). "Belief: Spontaneous and Reflective" *Pacific Philosophical Quarterly*, 68, 94–103.

————. (1987c). "Justification: Ethical and Epistemic," *Metaphilosophy*, 18, 187–99.

Moore, G. E. (1912). *Ethics* (London: Oxford University Press).

Moser, Paul. (1989). "Inferential Justification and Foley's Foundations," *Analysis*, 49, 84–88.

Nagel, Thomas. (1970). *The Possibility of Altruism* (Oxford: Oxford University Press).

Naylor, Margery B. (1985). "Voluntary Belief," *Philosophy and Phenomenological Research*, 45, 427–36.

Newman, Jay. (1986). *The Mental Philosophy of John Henry Newman* (Waterloo, Ontario: Wilfrid Laurier University Press).

Newman, Cardinal John Henry. (1978). *An Essay In Aid of a Grammar of Assent* (Notre Dame: University of Notre Dame Press).

Nozick, Robert. (1969). "Coercion," in Sidney Morgenbesser, ed., *Philosophy, Science and Method* (New York: Saint Martin's Press), 101–35.

O'Hear, Anthony. (1972). "Belief and the Will," *Philosophy*, 47, 95–112.

Pascal, Blaise. (1961). *Pensees*, J. M. Cohen, trans. (Baltimore: Penguin Books).

Plantinga, Alvin. (1983). "Reason and Belief in God," in Nicholas Wolterstorff and Alvin Plantinga, eds., *Faith and Rationality* (Notre Dame: University of Notre Dame Press), 16–93.

Pojman, Louis P. (1986). *Religious Belief and the Will* (London: Routledge and Kegan Paul).

Price, H. H. (1954). "Belief and the Will," *Proceedings of the Aristotelian Society*, Supplementary Volume 28, 1–22.

———. (1969). *Belief* (London: Allen and Unwin).

Prosser, William. (1971). "Negligence," reprinted in John Arthur and William Shaw, eds., *Readings of the Philosophy of Law* (Englewood Cliffs, NJ: Prentice–Hall, 1984), 318–26.

Quine, W.V.O. (1969). "Epistemology Naturalized," in *Ontological Relativity and Other Essays* (New York: Columbia University Press, 69–90.

———. (1990). *The Pursuit of Truth* (Cambridge, MA: Harvard University Press).

Roberts, Robert C. (1984). "Will Power and the Virtues," *Philosophical Review*, 93, 227–47.

Ryle, Gilbert. (1949). *The Concept of Mind* (New York: Barnes and Noble).

Sidgwick, Henry. (1907). "The Kantian Conception of Free Will," *The Methods of Ethics*, Appendix (London: Macmillan), 511–16.

Smith, Holly. (1983). "Culpable Ignorance," *The Philosophical Review*, 92, 543–71.

Sosa, Ernest. (1985). "Knowledge and Intellectual Virtue," *The Monist*, 68, 226–45.

———. (1991). "Intellectual Virtue in Perspective," in *Knowledge in Perspective* (Cambridge: Cambridge University Press).

Steup, Mathias. (1988). "The Deontic Conception of Epistemic Justification, *Philosophical Studies*, 53, 65–84.

Stevenson, J. T. (1975). "On Doxastic Responsibility," in Keith Lehrer, ed., *Analysis and Metaphysics* (Dordrecht: Reidel), 229–53.

Stich, Stephen. (1990). *The Fragmentation of Reason* (Cambridge, MA: MIT Press).

Sverdlik, Steven. (1991). "Culpable Negligence" (typescript).

Tlumak, Jeffrey. (1983). "Judgment and Understanding in Descartes's Philosophy," *Southern Journal of Philosophy*, 21, 89–99.

Von Wright, George Henrik. (1963). *Varieties of Goodness* (London: Routledge and Kegan Paul).

Wallace, James. (1978). *Virtues and Vices* (Ithaca, NY: Cornell University Press).

Watson, Gary. (1975). "Free Agency," *Journal of Philosophy*, 72, 205–20.

Williams, Bernard. (1973). "Deciding to Believe," in *Problems of the Self* (Cambridge: Cambridge University Press), 36–51.

———. (1978). *Descartes: The Project of Pure Enquiry* (London: Penguin Books).

Wilson, Margaret. (1978). *Descartes* (London: Routledge and Kegan Paul).

Wolf, Susan. (1980). "Asymmetrical Freedom," *Journal of Philosophy*, 77, 151–66.

Wolterstorff, Nicholas. (1983). "Can Belief in God Be Rational If It Has No Foundations?" in N. Wolterstorff and A. Plantinga, eds., *Faith and Rationality* (Notre Dame: University of Notre Dame Press), 135–86.

———. (1991). Review of Louis Pojman (1986), *Faith and Philosophy*, 7, 120–23.

Zimmerman, Michael J. (1988). *An Essay on Moral Responsibility* (Lanham, MD: Rowman and Littlefield).

Index

About the Author

James A. Montmarquet received his Ph.D. from the University of Chicago and is associate professor of philosophy at Tennessee State University in Nashville. He is the author of *The Idea of Agrarianism* (University of Idaho Press, 1989); his articles have appeared in such journals as the *American Philosophical Quarterly*, *The Journal of Philosophy*, *Mind*, *Analysis*, and *Philosophical Studies*.